TOP SECRET

TOP

WHEN OUR GOVERNMENT
KEEPS US IN THE DARK

SECRET

GEOFFREY R. STONE

ROWMAN & LITTLEFIELD PUBLISHERS, INC.

Lanham • Boulder • New York • Toronto • Plymouth, UK

ROWMAN & LITTLEFIELD PUBLISHERS, INC.

Published in the United States of America
by Rowman & Littlefield Publishers, Inc.
A wholly owned subsidiary of The Rowman & Littlefield Publishing Group, Inc.
4501 Forbes Boulevard, Suite 200, Lanham, Maryland 20706
www.rowmanlittlefield.com

Estover Road
Plymouth PL6 7PY
United Kingdom

British Library Cataloguing in Publication Information Available

Library of Congress Cataloging-in-Publication Data:

Stone, Geoffrey R.
    Top secret : when our government keeps us in the dark / Geoffrey R. Stone.
        p. cm. — (Free expression in America series)
    Includes bibliographical references and index.
    ISBN-13: 978-0-7425-5885-4 (cloth : alk. paper)
    ISBN-10: 0-7425-5885-1 (cloth : alk. paper)
    1. Freedom of information—United States. 2. Official secrets—United States.
    3. Freedom of the press—United States. I. Title. KF5753.S76 2007
    342.7308'53—dc22   2007016786

Printed in the United States of America

♾ ™ The paper used in this publication meets the minimum requirements of
American National Standard for Information Sciences—Permanence of Paper
for Printed Library Materials, ANSI/NISO Z39.48-1992.

A popular Government, without popular information,
or the means of acquiring it, is but a Prologue
to a Farce or a Tragedy; or perhaps both.

—**James Madison,** *The Writings of James Madison* (1822),
Gaillard Hunt, ed., G. P. Putnam's Sons, 1910

Contents

For Julie, Maddie & Jack

Acknowledgments

THIS book was initially conceived as part of a project of the First Amendment Center and was supported by the University of Chicago Law School's Frank Cicero Fund. I would like to thank Floyd Abrams, Scott Armstrong, Sandra Baron, Susan Buckley, Ronald Collins, Robert Corn-Revere, Lucy Dalglish, Harold Edgar, Lee Levine, Paul McMasters, Jeffrey Smith, and Stephen Vladeck for their participation in a very insightful discussion of the issues addressed in this book at a conference sponsored by the First Amendment Center, and I am especially grateful to Floyd Abrams, Harold Edgar, Louis Fisher, Lee Levine, Robert Post, Adam Samaha, and Stephen Schulhofer for their thoughtful comments on early drafts of this work. I am thankful to Alyssa Work for her proofreading. Various parts of this book were previously published as *Why We Need a Federal Reporter's Privilege*, 34 Hofstra Law Review 39 (2005), *Government Secrecy vs. Freedom of the Press*, 1 Harvard Law and Policy Review 185 (2007), and by the First Amendment Center as *Government Secrecy vs. Freedom of the Press*, 7 First Reports 1 (December 2006). Most of all, I want to thank Ronald Collins, who insisted I write this book and without whose persistence it would never have seen the light of day.

Foreword

THE tension between government secrecy and freedom of the press, so apparent today, is hardly new. One might even say that the very existence of such a tension is itself a mark of democracy—for where there is no tension there are fewer opportunities to strengthen national security and invigorate press freedom. Just how best to put that tension in the service of both ideals is the general subject of Professor Geoffrey Stone's book.

The words "sedition" and "espionage" connote disloyalty to one's country—the first by words or actions intended to harm or overthrow a nation, the second by spying or assisting spies to disseminate secret information in a way injurious to the national defense. Laws such as the Sedition Act of 1798,[1] the Espionage Act of 1917,[2] and the Sedition Act of 1918[3] thus raise an important question: To what extent can a free press fully and adequately inform the citizenry of the conduct of war—its course and costs—without actually jeopardizing military safety and national security? Or, phrased another way, how much of a watchdog role can the press play in wartime before its actions place our security at real risk?

"It is easy, by giving way to passion, intolerance, and suspicions in wartime," observed Justice Robert Jackson, "to reduce our liberties to a shadow, often in answer to exaggerated claims of security."[4] Then again, Justice Jackson also thought that caution should be taken lest our "constitutional Bill of Rights" become a "suicide pact."[5] These two takes on freedom point to the great difficulty in reconciling security, which is not counterfeit, with liberty, which is not destructive. That task is especially challenging when the wartime powers of the government clash with the wartime duties of a free and responsible press.

For Thomas I. Emerson, the renowned First Amendment scholar, sedition laws and the like are, "in the final analysis, a relic of government by monarchy. They are designed to destroy political opposition."[6] By that measure, nothing short of "overt action" harmful to national security may be punished. When such laws extend beyond that realm, he argued, "they cannot be reconciled with constitutional government."[7]

By contrast, several months before Congress passed the Sedition Act of 1918, the *Washington Post* editorialized that the proposed law, with its severe civil fines and criminal penalties, "will give the government full power to deal effectively with persons who are not in sympathy with the United States, and it is to be hoped that [when] it is written upon the statute books the Department of Justice will proceed with its enforcement." Any "superfluous concern for the right of free speech,"[8] the editors added, should not be allowed to stand in the way of vigorous enforcement of the act.

Zechariah Chafee, another free-speech scholar, looked at the matter through this lens: "The Espionage Act should not be construed to reverse [our] national policy of liberty of the press and silence hostile criticism, unless Congress had given the clearest expression of such an intention in the statute. Congress had no such intention in the Act of 1917."[9] Chafee likewise maintained that the First Amendment, as later interpreted by the Supreme Court, also restricted the government's power to employ espionage and sedition laws to abridge freedom of expression.[10]

If a line is to be drawn, where and why should it be drawn? That basic question was put to a group of scholars, lawyers, and journalists in a workshop held at the First Amendment Center on July 20, 2006. The participants in that five-hour workshop, which focused primarily on the Espionage Act and the press, were Floyd Abrams, Scott Armstrong, Sandra S. Baron, Susan Buckley, Shelby Coffey, Ronald K. L. Collins, Robert Corn-Revere, Lucy Dalglish, Harold S. H. Edgar, Lee Levine, Paul K. McMasters, Jeffrey H. Smith, Geoffrey R. Stone, and Stephen I. Vladeck.

Professor Stone agreed to prepare a working paper for the group and invited comments and criticisms. The goal was not to reach any consensus and incorporate such into the final report, but rather to critically discuss the subject and to present a variety of thoughts and options for him to consider. Hence, that report—now expanded into this book—reflected the informed conclusions of Professor Stone alone.

In preparation for the workshop, Professor Vladeck wrote a paper about the relevant statutory framework touching upon government secrecy and the press. That paper, too, was critically discussed and is published here in revised form to supplement Professor Stone's contribution. Here, again, it reflects the informed conclusions of its author alone. Additionally, the First Amendment Center's staff and research assistants prepared a timeline and an extended bibliography. My former colleague, Paul McMasters, was also a source of invaluable assistance.

Professor Stone wisely elected to supplement his original work with a chapter on the journalist-source privilege. Given the current importance of that topic, that addition will offer readers a yet richer consideration of the core issues addressed in *Top Secret.*

One of the purposes of the First Amendment is to prompt self-governing citizens to participate in informed discourse about the conduct of their government. In that spirit, the hope is that this book will enrich discussions among elected officials, judges, lawyers, educators, editors, reporters and, of course, civic-minded Americans. By that measure, *Top Secret* is a fitting work to launch the "Free Expression in America" series. Our aim, aided by our Editorial Advisors, is to secure future works of comparable high quality concerning a variety of timely free-speech topics.

Professor Geoffrey Stone's thoughtful writings remind us of something simple yet important: Those who surrender true liberty to a false security defend nothing worth preserving, while those who abandon real security to an illusory liberty protect nothing worth safeguarding.

—RONALD K. L. COLLINS

Notes

1. Act of July 14, 1798, ch. 74, 1 Stat. 596 (expired 1801).
2. Act of June 15, 1917, ch. 30, 40 Stat. 217 (18 U.S.C.§§ 793 et seq.).

3. Act of May 16, 1918, ch. 75, 40 Stat. 553 (repealed 1921).

4. Robert H. Jackson, "Wartime Security and Liberty under Law," 1 *Buffalo Law Review* 103, 116 (1951).

5. *Terminiello v. City of Chicago*, 337 U.S. 1, 37 (1949) (Jackson, J., dissenting).

6. Thomas I. Emerson, *The System of Freedom of Expression* (New York: Random House, 1970), 160.

7. Ibid.

8. Editorial, "To Suppress Disloyalists," *Washington Post* (January 18, 1918), 6.

9. Zechariah Chafee, Jr., *Free Speech in the United States* (Cambridge, MA: Harvard University Press, 1948), 44 (referring in part to Judge Learned Hand's opinion in *Masses Publishing Co. v. Patten*, 244 Fed. 535 (S.D.N.Y., 1917)).

10. See Chafee, supra at 108-140.

Introduction

SINCE September 11, 2001, the United States has investigated, threatened to prosecute, and prosecuted public employees, journalists, and the press for the dissemination of classified information relating to the national security. The government's response to the *New York Times*'s revelation of President George W. Bush's secret directive to the National Security Agency to engage in warrantless electronic surveillance illustrates the tension between the government and the press.

Several Republican members of Congress accused the *Times* of "treason," and 210 Republicans in the House of Representatives passed a resolution condemning the press for putting "the lives of Americans in danger." Attorney General Alberto Gonzales went so far as to suggest that the *Times* might be prosecuted for violating a provision of federal law making it a crime to disclose "information relating to the national defense" with "reason to believe" that the information "could be used to the injury of the United States."[1]

The government often has exclusive possession of information about its policies, programs, processes, and activities that would be of great value to informed public debate. In a self-governing society, citizens must know what their representatives are doing if they are intelligently to govern themselves. But government officials often insist that such information must be kept secret, even from those to whom they are accountable—the American people.

The reasons why public officials demand secrecy are many and varied. They range from the truly compelling to the patently illegitimate. Sometimes, government officials rightly fear that the disclosure of secret information would undermine the national security (for example, by revealing military secrets). Sometimes, they are concerned that the revelation of secret information would betray the confidences of citizens or other nations who provided the information on the assurance that it would remain confidential. Sometimes, public officials want to keep information secret because disclosure would expose to public view their own incompetence or wrongdoing.

The value of such information to informed public discourse varies widely. Sometimes, the information is extremely important to public debate (for example, the disclosure of unwise or even unlawful government programs or activities). Sometimes, the information is of no real value to public debate (for example, the disclosure of a non-newsworthy person's tax return or the identity of a non-newsworthy covert agent).

The most vexing conflicts arise when the public disclosure of a government secret is *both* harmful to the national security *and* valuable to self-governance. Suppose, for example, government officials conduct a study of the effectiveness of security measures at our nation's ports. The study concludes that many of our ports are vulnerable to terrorist attack. Should this study be kept secret or should it be disclosed to the public? On the one hand, publishing the report might endanger the nation by revealing our vulnerabilities to terrorists. On the other hand, its publication would alert the public to the situation, enable citizens to press government officials to remedy the problem, and empower the public to hold accountable those officials who failed to keep the nation safe. The public disclosure of such information could both cost and benefit the nation. Should the study be made public?

In theory, this question can be framed quite simply: Do the benefits outweigh the costs of disclosure? That is, does the value of the disclosure to informed public deliberation outweigh its danger to the national security? Unfortunately, as a practical matter, this simple framing of the issue is not very helpful. It is exceedingly difficult to measure in any objective, consistent, predictable, or coherent manner either the "value" of the disclosure to public discourse or its "danger" to the national security. And it is even more difficult to *balance* such incommensurables against one another. This might be the right question in theory, but it is an unmanageable question in practice. No system of government and no system of free expression could operate efficiently, consistently, or reliably if it is required to resolve that question every time it arises.

Moreover, even if we were to agree that this is the right question in theory, we would next have to determine *who* decides whether the benefits outweigh the costs of disclosure. Should this be decided by public officials whose responsibility it is to protect the national security? By public officials who might have an incentive to cover up their own mistakes? By lower-level public employees who believe their superiors are keeping information secret for inadequate reasons? By reporters, editors, and bloggers who have gained access to the information? By judges in the course of criminal prosecutions of leakers, journalists, and publishers?

Ultimately, *someone* has to decide whether public officials can keep such information secret and whether particular individuals can be discharged and/or criminally punished for leaking or publishing it. If we expect judges to decide these questions, how much deference should they give to public officials who claim that such disclosures endanger the national security? How much deference should they give to reporters, editors, and bloggers who claim that the disclosures are essential to informed public debate?

Interestingly, the American legal system almost never directly addresses the question whether the value of publication of confidential information outweighs the danger. Because that inquiry is so fraught with ambiguity, our legal system has devised a complex set of presumptions and doctrines, each addressing a distinctive element of the larger question. It is through the interaction of these presumptions and doctrines that we ultimately balance the national security against the right of the people to be informed.

In this volume, I explore whether the measures recently taken and suggested by the executive branch to prevent and punish the public disclosure of classified information are consistent with the First Amendment. I address four questions: (1) In what circumstances may the government discharge and/or criminally punish a public employee for disclosing classified information to a journalist for the purpose of publication?[2] (2) In what circumstances may the government criminally punish the press for publishing such information? (3) In what circumstances may the government criminally punish a journalist for receiving or soliciting such information from a government employee for the purpose of publication? (4) In what circumstances may the government compel a journalist to disclose the identity of the source of such information so it can criminally punish the source?

The issues are as difficult as they are important, and the governing law is often unformed and obscure. I shall try to bring clarity to these questions, which pose fundamental issues about the conflict between the government's need to keep secrets and the press's responsibility to inform the public and the government's accountability to its citizens.

Notes

1. 18 U.S.C. § 793(e). See also 18 U.S.C. § 798. After the *Times* disclosed the NSA spy program, Senator Pat Roberts of Kansas suggested that he might propose legislation expressly making it unlawful for nongovernment employees to communicate classified information. See Walter Pincus, "Senator May Seek Tougher Law on Leaks," *Washington Post* (Feb. 17, 2006), A1. Michael Barone, "Blowback on the Press," *U.S. News & World Report* (May 8, 2006); Rick Klein, "House Votes to Condemn Media Over Terror Story," *Boston Globe* (June 30, 2006), A1; David Remnick, "Nattering Nabobs," *New Yorker* (July 10, 2006), 33, 34. For a defense of the Bush administration's position, see Gabriel Schoenfeld, "Has the *New York Times* Violated the Espionage Act?," *Commentary* 23 (Mar. 2006). The *New York Times* won the Pulitzer Prize for journalism for publishing these stories.

2. Although I refer throughout the book to "classified" information, the basic principles I discuss would apply as well to information that is confidential but not classified. The fact of classification should be relevant to the analysis, but not dispositive of it. In other words, some confidential but not classified information might be so central to the national security that the government has a sufficient reason to protect it from public disclosure. There is also a problem when a journalist learns information orally, without receiving a copy of a source document. In that situation, the journalist will not see the classification on the document, which might lead to factual questions about the journalist's knowledge at the time he received the information.

Government Employees

I BEGIN with individuals who are *not* government employees. In what circumstances may such persons be held legally accountable for revealing information to a journalist for the purpose of publication? The answer to this question will enable us to establish a baseline definition of First Amendment rights. I will then inquire whether the rights of government employees are any different.[1]

Freedom to Share Information

In general, an individual, who is not a government employee, has a broad First Amendment right to reveal information to a journalist for the purpose of publication. There are a few limitations, however.

First, the Supreme Court has long recognized that there are "certain well defined and narrowly limited classes of speech," such as false statements of fact, obscenity, and threats, that "are no essential part of any exposition of ideas and are of such slight social value as a step to truth that any benefit that may be derived from them is clearly outweighed by the social interest in order and morality."[2] Because such categories of speech have "low" First Amendment value, they may be restricted without satisfying the usual demands of the First Amendment.[3]

For example, if X makes a knowingly false and defamatory statement about Y to a journalist, with the understanding that the journalist will publish the information, X might be liable to Y for the tort of defamation. Or, if X reveals to a reporter that Y was raped, with the expectation that the reporter will publish the information, X might be liable to Y for invasion of privacy. The public disclosure of Y's identity, unlike the fact of the rape, might be thought to be of such slight value to public debate that it can be prohibited in order to protect Y's privacy.[4]

Second, private individuals sometimes voluntarily contract with other private individuals to limit their speech. Violation of such a private agreement might be actionable as a breach of contract. For example, if X takes a job as a salesman and agrees as a condition of employment not to disclose his employer's customer list to competitors, he might be liable for breach of contract if he reveals the list to a reporter for a trade journal with the expectation that the journal will publish the list. Or, if Y accepts employment as a chemist and agrees not to disclose her company's trade secrets, she might be liable for breach of contract if she reveals the information to a journalist. In these circumstances, the individual has voluntarily agreed to limit what otherwise would be a First Amendment right. Such privately negotiated waivers of constitutional rights are usually enforceable.[5]

Third, there might be situations, however rare, in which an individual discloses previously nonpublic information to a journalist in circumstances in which publication of the information would be so dangerous to society that the individual might be punished for disclosing it to the journalist. For example, suppose a scientist discovers how to produce the ebola virus from ordinary household materials. The harm caused by the public dissemination of that information might be so likely, imminent, and grave that the scientist could be punished for facilitating its publication.[6]

These examples illustrate the few circumstances in which an individual might be held legally responsible for disclosing information to a journalist for the purpose of publication. In general, however, the First Amendment accords individuals very broad freedom to share information with reporters for the purpose of publication.

Limitations on Public Employees' Speech

To what extent is a *government employee* in a similar position? When we ask about the First Amendment rights of public employees, we must focus on the second of the three situations examined above. It is the waiver-of-rights issue that poses the critical question. Although the first and third situations are relevant in the public employee context, it is the waiver issue that is at the core of the matter.

At first blush, it might seem that, whatever might be the case with private employers, the government cannot constitutionally insist that individuals surrender their First Amendment rights as a condition of public employment. Surely, it would be unconstitutional, for example, for the government to require individuals to agree as a condition of employment that they will never criticize the president, practice the Muslim faith, or assert their constitutional right to be free from unreasonable searches and seizures. It would be no answer for the government to point out that the individuals had voluntarily agreed not to criticize the president, practice their faith, or assert their Fourth Amendment rights, for even if individuals consent to surrender their constitutional rights in order to obtain a government job, the government cannot constitutionally condition employment on the waiver of those rights. As the Supreme Court has long held, "unconstitutional conditions" on public employment violate the Constitution. The government cannot legitimately use its leverage over jobs, welfare benefits, driver's licenses, tax deductions, zoning waivers, and the like to extract waivers of constitutional rights.[7]

One might argue that because *private* employers can constitutionally extract concessions from their employees as a condition of employment, including waivers of what would otherwise be constitutional rights, the government should be able to do the same. There are three answers to this argument. First, the Constitution does not bind private employers. It binds only the government. Second, the government's scale and power are so vast that it can have a much more pervasive impact on individual freedom than private employers. Third, because government is not profit-driven, it is much more likely than private employers to sacrifice economic efficiency in order to achieve other, especially political, goals. The government, for example, is much more likely than private employers to refuse to hire people who do not support the party in power, thus leveraging government power for political advantage.[8]

This does not mean, however, that the government may *never* require individuals to waive their constitutional rights as a condition of public employment. There are at least two circumstances, relevant to the issue under consideration, in which the government may restrict the First Amendment rights of its employees. First, as the Supreme Court noted in *Pickering v. Board of Education*, the government

> has interests as an employer in regulating the speech of its employees that differ significantly from those it possesses in connection with regulation of the speech of the citizenry in general. The problem in any case is to arrive at a balance between the interests of the [public employee], as a citizen, in commenting upon matters of public concern and the interest of the [government], as an employer, in promoting the efficiency of the public services it performs through its employees.[9]

The government has a legitimate interest in running efficiently, and some restrictions of employee speech might be reasonably necessary to achieve that efficiency. The Hatch Act, for instance, prohibits public employees from taking an active part in political campaigns. The goal is to insulate public employees from undue political pressure and improper influence. To enable public employees to perform their jobs properly, the government may require them to waive what would otherwise be the First Amendment right to participate in partisan political activities.[10]

Another illustration might involve a police officer who uses racist language in a street encounter. In such circumstances, the police department might reasonably conclude that the officer can no longer perform her job effectively or that her continued employment would seriously undermine the department's credibility with the community. As *Pickering* observed, it may be appropriate in such circumstances to "balance" the competing interests.

Similarly, a government employee's disclosure of confidential information to a journalist for the purpose of publication might jeopardize the government's ability to function effectively. For example, if an IRS employee gives a reporter X's confidential tax records, this might seriously impair the public's confidence in the tax system and thus undermine the government's capacity to function efficiently.[11]

A second reason why the government may sometimes restrict what otherwise would be the First Amendment rights of public employees is that the employee learns the information *only* by virtue of his government employment. Arguably, it is one thing for the government to prohibit its employees from speaking in ways other citizens can speak, but something else entirely for it to prohibit them from speaking in ways other citizens *cannot* speak. If a public employee gains access to confidential information only because of his public employment, then prohibiting him from disclosing that information to anyone outside the government might be said not to restrict his First Amendment rights at all, because he had no right to know the information in the first place.[12] The presence of this factor adds weight to the government's side of the *Pickering* balance.

There is little clear law on this question. In *Snepp v. United States*,[13] however, the Supreme Court held that a former employee of the CIA could constitutionally be held to his agreement not to publish "any information or material relating to the Agency, its activities or intelligence activities generally, either during or after the term of [his] employment, [without] specific prior approval by the Agency." The Court did not suggest that every government employee can be required to abide by such a rule. Rather, it emphasized that a "former intelligence agent's publication of . . . material relating to intelligence activities can be detrimental to vital national interests."[14]

In light of *Snepp* and *Pickering*, it seems reasonable to assume that a public employee who discloses classified information relating to the national security to a journalist for the purpose of publication has violated his position of trust and ordinarily may be discharged and/or criminally punished without violating the First Amendment.

It is important to note that this conclusion is specific to public employees. It does not govern those who are *not* public employees. Unlike public employees who have agreed to abide by constitutionally permissible restrictions of their speech, journalists and publishers have not agreed to waive their rights. The analogy is to the private employee who agrees not to disclose his employer's customer lists. Although he might be liable for breach of contract, the journalist to whom he discloses the list and the trade journal that publishes it are not liable to the employer.[15]

Moreover, as the Court recognized in *Pickering*, the government has greater (though not unlimited) need to restrict the speech of its employees than to restrict the speech of individuals generally. This is because the government's interests in regulating the speech of its employees are different from its interests in regulating speech generally. The government cannot constitutionally punish individuals for making racist comments, but it can discipline a police officer who makes such comments on the job.

The distinction between public employees and other individuals is critical in the context of confidential information. Information the government wants to keep secret may be of great value to the public. The public disclosure of an individual's tax return may undermine the public's confidence in the tax system, but it may also reveal important information about a political candidate's finances. The conclusion that the government has a legitimate reason to prohibit its employees from disclosing such information does not reflect a judgment that the government's interest in confidentiality *outweighs* the public's interest in disclosure. Indeed, information about a political candidate's finances might be of fundamental significance to public debate. It would plainly be unconstitutional for the government to prohibit the dissemination of such information if it did not come from the government's own files.

In theory, of course, it would be possible for courts to decide in each instance whether an unauthorized disclosure of confidential information by a public employee is protected by the First Amendment because the value of the information to the public outweighs the government's need for secrecy. But such an approach would put courts in an extremely awkward position and would in effect convert the First Amendment into a constitutional Freedom of Information Act. The Supreme Court has sensibly eschewed that approach and granted the government considerable deference in deciding whether and when public employees may disclose confidential government information.[16]

Disclosure of Classified Information

Such disclosures are not always punishable, however. In applying *Pickering* and *Snepp*, courts do not give the government carte blanche to insist on secrecy. The government's restrictions must be reasonable.

Returning to the problem of confidential information relating to the national security, I begin with classified information. The existing classification system authorizes public employees to classify any information the unauthorized disclosure of which could reasonably be expected to harm the national security. Access to such information is restricted to individuals with an appropriate security clearance. A government employee may not disclose such information to any person who is not authorized to know it.[17]

The classification system is a highly imperfect guide to the *need* for confidentiality. The concept "reasonably be expected to harm the national security" is inherently vague and plastic. It is impossible to know from this standard how likely, imminent, or grave the potential harm must actually be. Moreover, the classification process is poorly designed and sloppily implemented. Predictably, the government tends to overclassify information. An employee charged with the task of classifying information inevitably will err on the side of over- rather than underclassification. No employee wants to be responsible for underclassification. In addition, we know from experience that public officials have often abused the classification system to hide from public scrutiny their own misjudgments, incompetence, and venality.[18]

Despite these very real concerns, there is good reason to have clear, simple, and easily administered rules to guide public employees. Hence, a government employee ordinarily can be disciplined, discharged, or prosecuted for knowingly disclosing classified information to a journalist for the purpose of publication.[19]

Requirements for Punishing Disclosure

Are there any circumstances in which a public employee has a First Amendment right to disclose classified information to a journalist for the purpose of publication? Courts have recognized two conditions that must be satisfied in order for the government to criminally punish the employee. First, the government must prove that the disclosure would be "potentially damaging to the United States."[20] Although this judgment is implicit in the very fact of classification, the fact of classification is not conclusive. Because the classification process is imperfect, the courts require independent proof of at least potential harm to the national security.

Second, the government must prove that it has attempted to keep the information secret and that the information was in fact secret before the employee's disclosure. As Judge Learned Hand noted more than sixty years ago, "it is obviously lawful" for a public employee to reveal information that the government has not withheld from the public.[21] The government must prove that the information was "closely held" and "not available to the general public" prior to the disclosure.[22]

Thus, to prosecute a public employee for disclosing classified information to a reporter, the government must prove that the information was not already in the public domain and that the disclosure was potentially damaging to the national security.

This is a far cry from requiring the government to prove that the employee knew the disclosure would create a likely and imminent danger of grave harm to the nation (the standard suggested earlier in the ebola example). The gap between these two standards represents the difference between the rights of ordinary individuals and the rights of public employees. This gap represents what the public employee surrenders as a condition of his employment; it is the effect of *Pickering* balancing; and it is a measure of the deference we grant to government in the management of its "internal" affairs.[23]

Under this approach, that the classification of a particular document might have been erroneous is not in itself sufficient justification for a public employee to breach his contract with the government. A public employee does not have a First Amendment right to second-guess the classification system. As long as the conditions of potential harm and prior secrecy are satisfied, the employee has no constitutional right to disclose classified information and then assert in his defense that the information was insufficiently dangerous or too valuable to public debate to justify the government's decision to keep it secret. A central goal of the classification system is to avoid such ad hoc judgments, and courts generally should not be in the business of second-guessing the classifiers.[24]

This approach is obviously problematic. As we have seen, the disclosure of confidential information may be *both* harmful to the national security *and* valuable to public debate. Consider, for example, information relating to (a) secret understandings with other nations, (b) evaluations of new weapons systems, (c) plans for shooting down hijacked airplanes, (d) evaluations of the adequacy of private industry's protection of nuclear power plants, and (e) government policies on the use of torture. One might reasonably conclude that some or all of this information should be available to the public to enable informed public deliberation. But the approach to public employees outlined above clearly empowers the government to forbid the disclosure of such information.

Thus, granting a high level of deference to the government to determine what information to withhold from the public significantly *overprotects* government secrecy at the expense of both official accountability and informed public debate. There is no reason to believe that government officers will reach the "right" result in striking the balance between secrecy and disclosure. Not only do they have powerful incentives to overclassify, but the classification standard itself considers only one side of the balance—whether disclosure might harm the national security. It does not even take into account the other side of the balance—whether disclosure might enhance democratic governance. This is the price we pay for a simple, easy-to-administer rule for public employees.

Disclosure of Unlawful Government Activity

There is at least one situation, however, in which a government employee *must* have a First Amendment right to disclose classified information. This arises when the disclosure reveals *unlawful* government conduct.

Applying the *Pickering* standard, the government has no legitimate interest in keeping secret its own illegality, and the public has a compelling interest in the disclosure of such information. Even if the government ordinarily can punish a public employee for disclosing classified information, that presumption disappears when the disclosure reveals the government's own wrongdoing. The government is, after all, accountable to the public. In a self-governing society, citizens need to know when their representatives violate the law.[25]

Even in this situation, the government might argue that public employees should *never* disclose classified information—even if the disclosure reveals unlawful government conduct. After all, even a well-intentioned "whistle-blower" might be wrong in his assessment of a program's legality, and by disclosing the information might seriously damage the national security. The government might argue that, at least in dealing with classified information, government employees must err on the side of protecting the national security and that such "leakers" must be punished, even if the program is unlawful. Only in this way, the government might argue, can it effectively deter future leakers from playing craps with the national security.

From a constitutional perspective, this is unexplored terrain. But in my judgment, the government employee must prevail on this issue. In terms of deterrence, it should suffice for the government to punish those who disclose classified programs that are not unlawful. When the program is in fact unlawful, the public's need to know outweighs the government's interest in secrecy. As we have seen, public employees cannot be criminally punished for disclosing classified information that is already public or whose disclosure does not pose a threat to the national security. Public employees who disclose government illegality should have similar protection.

An intermediate position might allow the government to punish public employees who disclose even unlawful programs if (a) the employee knew that the government regards the program's secrecy as critical to the national security, and (b) there are reasonable procedures in place through which the employee could question the legality of the program, without going to the press, and he fails to use those procedures.[26] If such procedures exist and the employee complies with them, he should not be punishable for then disclosing an unlawful program.

A related question is whether a public employee can be punished for disclosing a classified program she reasonably but *wrongly* believed to be unlawful. A familiar analogy resolves this problem. If an individual reasonably believes that a criminal law restricting speech violates the First Amendment, she may violate the law and raise the constitutional issue as a defense. If she was right in believing the law unconstitutional, she cannot be punished. But if she was wrong, she can be convicted, because the First Amendment does not recognize as a defense the defendant's reasonable belief that the law was invalid. This same principle should apply to public employees who disclose classified information.

To summarize: A public employee who knowingly discloses classified information to a journalist for the purpose of publication may be criminally punished if the information was not already in the public domain and its disclosure has the potential to harm the national security, *unless* the disclosure reveals unlawful government action and the employee has complied with reasonable whistle-blower procedures governing the disclosure of such information.[27]

Notes

1. Although this section focuses on government employees, a similar analysis would apply to government contractors who are granted access to national security information. See *Board of County Commissioners, Wabaunsee County, Kansas v. Umbehr*, 518 U.S. 668 (1996) (private contractors have same First Amendment rights as public employees); *O'Hare Truck Service, Inc. v. City of Northlake*, 518 U.S. 712 (1996) (same).

2. *Chaplinsky v. New Hampshire*, 315 U.S. 568, 571-72 (1942).

3. See *Roth v. United States*, 354 U.S. 476 (1957) (obscenity); *Gertz v. Robert Welch, Inc.*, 418 U.S. 323 (1974) (false statements of fact); *Central Hudson Gas v. Public Service Comm'n of New York*, 447 U.S. 557 (1980) (commercial advertising); *Virginia v. Black*, 538 U.S. 343 (2003) (threats).

4. This is a more speculative example than defamation, because the Supreme Court has never upheld either a criminal prosecution or civil liability for invasion of privacy by publication. See *Cox Broadcasting v. Cohn*, 420 U.S. 469 (1975) (broadcaster cannot be held liable in damages for publishing a rape victim's name where the name was lawfully obtained by examining a copy of the indictment); *Florida Star v. B.J.F.*, 491 U.S. 524 (1989) (reversing the judgment that found a newspaper civilly liable for publishing a rape victim's name that was publicly available); *Oklahoma Publishing Co. v. District Court*, 430 U.S. 308 (1977) (reporter cannot be prohibited from disclosing the name of a juvenile offender where the name was obtained at court proceedings that were open to the public); *Smith v. Daily Mail Publishing Co.*, 443 U.S. 97 (1979) (newspaper cannot be punished for publishing the name and photograph of a juvenile offender where the newspaper had learned the suspect's name from several witnesses to the shooting and from police and prosecutors at the scene).

5. See *Cohen v. Cowles Media Co.*, 501 U.S. 663 (1991) (confidential source can sue reporter for promissory estoppel for disclosing his identity in violation of the reporter's promise not to do so).

6. A somewhat analogous situation was arguably presented in *United States v. The Progressive*, 467 F. Supp. 990 (W.D. Wis. 1979) (granting an injunction against publication of an article in a magazine allegedly providing information about how to make a nuclear bomb).

7. See, e.g., *Perry v. Sinderman*, 408 U.S. 593, 597 (1972) ("even though a person has no 'right' to a valuable government benefit and even though the government may deny him the benefit for any number of reasons," it may not do so "on a basis that infringes his constitutionally protected interests—especially his interest in freedom of speech").

8. Cass Sunstein has put the point well:

> Citizens may often find it in their interest to give up rights of free speech in exchange for benefits from government. . . . But if government is permitted to obtain enforceable waivers, the aggregate effect may be considerable, and the deliberative processes of the public will be skewed. . . . Waivers of first amendment rights thus affect people other than government employees, and effects on third parties are a classic reason to proscribe waivers. The analogy [is] to government purchases of voting rights, which are impermissible even if voters willingly assent.

Cass R. Sunstein, "Government Control of Information," 74 *Cal. L. Rev.* 889, 915 (1986).

9. 391 U.S. 563, 568 (1968).

10. See *U.S. Civil Service Commission v. National Association of Letter Carriers*, 413 U.S. 548 (1973); *United States Workers v. Mitchell*, 330 U.S. 75 (1947).

11. See also *Connick v. Meyers*, 461 U.S. 138 (1983) (*Pickering* does not apply to public employee speech relating only to matters of personal interest); *Rankin v. McPherson*, 483 U.S. 378 (1987) (*Pickering* applies to speech relating to matters of public concern).

12. See *Seattle Times Co. v. Rhinehart*, 467 U.S. 20 (1984) (upholding a protective order prohibiting a newspaper from publishing confidential information it obtained through discovery because the newspaper gained access to the information only "by virtue of the trial court's discovery processes"). See also Robert C. Post, "The Management of Speech: Discretion and Rights," 1984, *Supreme Court Review*, 169.

13. 444 U.S. 507 (1980).

14. Id., at 511. See also *Haig v. Agee*, 453 U.S. 280 (1981) (upholding the Secretary of State's revocation of a former CIA employee's passport for exposing the identities of covert CIA agents).

15. See also *Gentile v. State Bar of Nevada*, 501 U.S. 1030, 1074 (1991) (the extrajudicial "speech of lawyers representing clients in pending cases may be regulated under a less demanding standard than that established for regulation of the press," because lawyers are voluntary participants in the legal system); *Landmark Communications, Inc. v. Virginia*, 435 U.S. 829 (1978) (government may not punish the press for publishing confidential information, even though it may prohibit public employees from disclosing that information); *Nebraska Press Association v. Stuart*, 427 U.S. 539 (1976) (government may not restrain the press from publishing information about a criminal defendant, even though it may prohibit public employees from disclosing such information to the press).

16. For an excellent critique of this conclusion, see Adam M. Samaha, "Government State Secrets, Constitutional Law, and Platforms for Judicial Intervention," 53 *U.C.L.A. L. Rev.* 909, 948-976 (2006) (suggesting that the Freedom of Information Act can provide a useful "platform" for recognizing and enforcing a broader constitutional right of access to government secrets).

17. See Executive Order No. 13,292, 68 Fed. Reg. 15,315 (March 25, 2003), *amending* Executive Order No. 12,958, 60 Fed. Reg. 19,825 (April 17, 1995). There are three designations. "Top Secret" refers to information the unauthorized disclosure of which could reasonably be expected to cause exceptionally grave damage to the national security. "Secret" refers to information the unauthorized disclosure of which could reasonably be expected to cause serious damage to the national security. "Confidential" applies to information the authorized disclosure of which could reasonably be expected to cause damage to the national security. See id. at 15,326.

18. See, e.g., *United States v. Morison*, 844 F.2d 1057, 1081 (4th Cir. 1988) (Wilkinson, J., concurring) ("[t]here exists a tendency, even in a constitutional democracy, for government to withhold reports of disquieting developments and to manage news in a fashion most favorable to itself"); *Halperin v. Kissinger*, 606 F.2d 1192, 1204 n.77 (D.C. Cir. 1979) (noting "the well-documented practice of classifying as confidential much relatively innocuous or noncritical information"). See also, Harold Edgar and Benno Schmidt, Jr., "Curtiss-Wright Comes Home: Executive Power and National Security Secrecy," 21 *Harv. C.R.-C.L. L. Rev.* 349, 354 (1986) (the "[e]xecutive is inherently self-interested in expanding the scope of matters deemed 'secret'; the more that is secret, the more that falls under executive control"). By the mid-1990s, 1,336 government employees were authorized to classify information "top secret," and more than two million public employees and one million government contractors had "derivative classification" authority. See *Report of the Commission on Protecting and Reducing Government Secrecy*, xxxix, Sen.Doc. 105-2, 103rd Cong. (Government Printing Office, 1997) (Chairman's Statement).

19. What if a public employee discloses to a journalist information relating to the national security that is not classified? One approach would be to hold that nonclassification is dispositive. But such an approach would not work when what is being disclosed is information that is not itself in tangible form and therefore cannot be marked as "classified." An alternative approach is to allow the government to punish the disclosure by a public employee of nonclassified information if the employee knew both that the government regarded the information as confidential and that the unauthorized disclosure of the information could be expected to cause damage to the national security. See *United States v. Rosen*, Case No. 1:05cr225 (E.D. Va., August 9, 2006).

20. *United States v. Morison*, 844 F.2d 1057, 1071-1072 (4th Cir. 1988); *United States v. Rosen*, Case No. 1:05cr225 p. 25 (E.D. Va. August 9, 2006).

21. *United States v. Heine*, 151 F.2d 813, 817 (2d Cir. 1945). *Cf. Cox Broadcasting Corp. v. Cohn*, 420 U.S. 469 (1975); *The Florida Star v. B. J. F.*, 491 U.S. 524 (1989).

22. *United States v. Morison*, 844 F. 2d 1057, 1071-72 (4th Cir. 1988); *United States v. Rosen*, at 23-24. See *United States v. Truong Din Hung*, 629 F.2d 908, 918 n.9 (4th Cir. 1980); *United States v. Allen*, 31 M.J. 572, 627-28 (N.C.M.R. 1987).

23. For examples of cases dealing with public employees in the context of classified information, see *United States v. Morison*, 844 F.2d 1057 (4th Cir. 1988); *United States v. Zettl*, 835 F.2d 1059 (4th Cir. 1987); *United States v. Kampiles*, 609 F.2d 1233 (7th Cir. 1980); *United States v. Marchetti*, 466 F.2d 1309 (4th Cir. 1972).

24. This is similar to the tax return situation. An IRS employee does not have a constitutional right to leak an otherwise confidential tax return because the confidentiality of that return is not sufficiently "important" to warrant confidentiality.

25. Indeed, federal law forbids classification for the purpose of concealing "violations of law, inefficiency, or administrative error." Executive Order No. 13,292, § 1.7(a)(1), 68 Fed. Reg. 15315 (Mar. 25, 2003).

26. The Intelligence Community Whistleblower Protection Act of 1998 sets forth a limited mechanism to enable whistle-blowers dealing with classified information to raise their concerns with agency officials or members of congressional oversight committees. The act covers whistle-blowers who want to report (1) a serious abuse or violation of law; (2) a false statement to, or willful withholding of information from, Congress; or (3) a reprisal in response to an employee's reporting of an urgent matter.

27. On August 2, 2006, Senator Christopher Bond introduced legislation to clarify the circumstances in which public employees or others who are officially entrusted with access to classified information may be criminally prosecuted for unauthorized disclosure of such information. The proposed legislation would make it unlawful for such persons knowingly to disclose classified information to any person who is not authorized to receive it. The proposal defines "classified information" as information or material that has been "properly classified." This law would clearly apply to disclosures to members of the press. Whether this law would be constitutional depends on the interpretation of "properly classified." The proposal would, in my view, be constitutional if "properly classified" is construed as excluding the classification of information already in the public domain, information whose disclosure does not have the potential to harm the national security, and information that reveals unlawful government action. Congress enacted similar legislation in 2000, but President Bill Clinton vetoed it as unconstitutional under the First Amendment. See www.fas.org/sgp/news/2006/08/bond080206.html; www.fas.org/irp/congress/2006_cr/s3774.html.

The Press

IN what circumstances may the government criminally punish the press for publishing classified information? In the entire history of the United States, the government has never prosecuted the press for publishing confidential information relating to the national security. Of course, this does not mean such a prosecution is impossible. It may be that the press has exercised great restraint and has never published confidential information in circumstances in which a prosecution would be constitutionally permissible. Or, it may be that the government has exercised great restraint and has never prosecuted the press even though such prosecutions would have been constitutionally permissible. We cannot know the answer until we define the circumstances in which such a prosecution would be consistent with the First Amendment.[1]

The Pentagon Papers Controversy

Because there has never been such a prosecution, the Supreme Court has never had occasion to rule on such a case. The closest it has come to such a situation was *New York Times v. United States*,[2] the Pentagon Papers case.

In 1967, Secretary of Defense Robert McNamara commissioned a top-secret study of the Vietnam War. The study, which filled forty-seven volumes, reviewed in great detail the formulation of United States policy toward Indochina, including military operations and secret diplomatic negotiations. In the spring of 1970, Daniel Ellsberg, a former Defense

Department official, gave a copy of the Pentagon Papers to the *New York Times*. On June 13, the *Times* began publishing excerpts from the papers. The next day, Attorney General John Mitchell sent a telegram to the publisher of the *Times* stating that its publication of this material was "prohibited" by federal law and that further publication would "cause irreparable injury to the defense interests of the United States." He therefore requested that the *Times* "publish no further information of this character and advise" him that it had "made arrangements for the return of these documents to the Department of Defense."

Two hours later, the *Times* transmitted a response, which it released publicly: "The *Times* must respectfully decline the request of the Attorney General, believing that it is in the interest of the people of this country to be informed of the material contained in this series of articles." The *Times* added that if the government sought to enjoin any further publication of the material, it would contest the government's position, but would "abide by the final decision of the court."[3]

Events escalated quickly. On June 15, the United States filed a complaint for injunction against the *Times*. The federal district court promptly granted the government's request for a temporary restraining order on the ground that "any temporary harm that may result from not publishing during the pendency of the application for a preliminary injunction is far outweighed by the irreparable harm that could be done to the interests of the United States government if it should ultimately prevail" in the case.[4] This was the first time in the history of the United States that a federal judge had restrained a newspaper from publishing information relevant to public debate.

Over the next few days, the matter rapidly worked its way up to the Supreme Court. On June 30, the Court announced its decision. Reflecting the unprecedented nature of the case, each justice wrote an opinion. Six justices held that the government had not met its "heavy burden of showing justification" for a prior restraint on the press. The Court therefore ruled that the *Times* was free to resume publication of the Pentagon Papers.

Justice Potter Stewart's opinion best captures the view of the Court: "We are asked . . . to prevent the publication . . . of material that the Executive Branch insists should not, in the national interest, be published. I am convinced that the Executive is correct with respect to some of the documents involved. But I cannot say that disclosure of any of them will surely result in direct, immediate, and irreparable damage to our Nation or its people."[5]

Different Standards for the Press Than for Public Employees

A fundamental question posed by the Pentagon Papers controversy is *who* should decide whether classified information should be made public. In the first instance, it would seem that our elected officials, who are charged with the responsibility of protecting the national security, must have the authority to decide such matters. But we know that our elected officials may sometimes have mixed motives for keeping secrets. They may be concerned not only with protecting the national security, but also with covering up their own mistakes, misjudgments, and wrongdoing. To give them the final say would risk depriving the American people of critical information about the conduct of their elected officials.

In the Pentagon Papers case, the Supreme Court held that although elected officials have broad authority to keep classified information secret, once that information gets into the hands of the press the government has only very limited authority to prevent its further dissemination. This may seem an awkward, even incoherent, state of affairs. If the government can constitutionally prohibit public employees from disclosing classified information to the press in the first place, why can't it enjoin the press from publishing that information if a government employee unlawfully discloses it?

But one could just as easily flip the question. If the press has a First Amendment right to publish classified information unless publication will "surely result in direct, immediate, and irreparable damage to our Nation or its people," why should the government be allowed to prohibit its employees from revealing such information to the press merely because it poses a potential danger to the national security? If we view the issue from the perspective of either the public's right to know or the government's interest in secrecy, it would seem logically that the same rule should apply to both public employees and the press. The very different standards governing public employees, on the one hand, and the press, on the other, presents a puzzle.

There are good reasons for this state of affairs. As we have seen, the government has broad authority to prohibit public employees from disclosing classified information to the press. This rule is based not on a careful balancing of the government's need for secrecy versus the public's need for information, but on a combination of the employee's consent to this limitation of his freedoms and the government's reasonable desire for a clear, easily administrable rule for public employees. For the sake of efficiency and simplicity, the law governing public employees substantially overprotects the government's legitimate interest in secrecy. But the employee's consent and the need for a simple rule for public employees have nothing to do with the rights of the press or the needs of the public. Under ordinary First Amendment standards, the press has broad freedom to publish information of value to public debate unless, at the very least, the government can prove that the publication poses a clear and present danger of serious harm.[6]

As the Yale constitutional scholar Alexander Bickel once observed, this may seem a "disorderly situation." But if we grant the government too much power to punish the press, we risk too great a sacrifice of public deliberation; if we give the government too little power to control confidentiality "at the source," we risk too great a sacrifice of secrecy.[7] The solution is to reconcile the irreconcilable values of secrecy and accountability by guaranteeing both a strong authority of the government to prohibit leaks and an expansive right of the press to publish them.[8] This balance may seem awkward in theory and unruly in practice, but it has stood the test of time.[9]

Prior Restraint vs. Criminal Prosecution

Three questions remain: (1) Does the same constitutional standard govern criminal prosecutions and prior restraints? (2) What disclosures might satisfy the Pentagon Papers standard? (3) What about information that both satisfies the Pentagon Papers standard and contributes to public debate?

In the Pentagon Papers case, the Supreme Court emphasized that it was dealing with a prior restraint, a type of speech restriction that bears a particularly "heavy presumption against its constitutional validity." This raises the question whether the test stated in Pentagon Papers governs criminal prosecutions as well as prior restrains. The inquiry is important, because Justices White and Stewart intimated in Pentagon Papers that this was an open question.[10]

The concept of prior restraint is deeply embedded in the history of the First Amendment. Historically, censorship took the form of licensing. No one could publish without first obtaining a license from the government. Anyone who published without obtaining a license could be punished, even if he could prove that he would have been issued a license. The failure to comply with the system was itself a crime.

Injunctions operate in much the same way. If a publication is enjoined, and a publisher violates the injunction, he can be punished for violating the injunction, even if the injunction was improperly granted. In this sense, licensing requirements and injunctions are different from ordinary criminal laws. A speaker who is prosecuted for violating a criminal law can assert the defense that the law is unconstitutional. Licensing schemes and injunctions, on the other hand, cannot be challenged in this manner. They are ordinarily governed by the "collateral bar rule," which provides that they can be challenged only by appealing the issuance of the injunction or the denial of the license. As a consequence, injunctions and licensing requirements are arguably more likely than criminal statutes to induce compliance with their terms, at least for the time it takes to appeal.[11]

On the other hand, the penalties for violating a licensing requirement or an injunction are usually much less severe than those for violating a criminal law, and a system of prior restraint actually has the virtue of enabling the speaker to know in advance whether his speech is subject to punishment. As a consequence, the logic of the prior restraint doctrine has often been questioned. As the Harvard law professor Paul Freund observed more than fifty years ago, "it will hardly do to place 'prior restraint' in a special category for condemnation."[12]

Whatever one thinks of the prior-restraint doctrine, its primary significance involves issues like obscenity and libel. When the government regulates low-value speech, it ordinarily may do so on the basis of a relatively undemanding standard. In that setting, the demanding test applied to prior restraints has real bite.[13] But in dealing with expression that lies at the very heart of the First Amendment—speech about the conduct of government itself—the distinction between prior restraint and criminal prosecution carries much less weight.

The Supreme Court has made clear that the government ordinarily may not criminally punish speech about public affairs because of its content unless, at the very least, it creates a clear and present danger of serious harm. Although the precise words may differ from one case to another, the basic elements of the test are the same. Thus, as a practical matter, the standard used in Pentagon Papers is essentially the same as the standard the Court would use in a criminal prosecution of the press for publishing information about the activities of government.[14] Indeed, in the thirty-five years since the Pentagon Papers case, the Supreme Court has not once upheld a content-based criminal prosecution of truthful speech relating to the activities of government that did not involve some special circumstance, such as public employment. That, in itself, speaks volumes. I conclude that the test articulated in Pentagon Papers is essentially the standard the Court would have applied in a criminal prosecution of the *Times* for publishing the Pentagon Papers. And even if that was not obvious in 1971, it seems clear today.[15]

Criminal Punishment for the Publication of Classified Information

What is an example of information the publication of which could be criminally punished? The traditional example was "the sailing dates of transports" or the "location of troops" in wartime.[16] In some circumstances, the publication of such information could instantly alert the enemy and endanger American lives. There might be little the government could do to protect our sailors and soldiers from attack. Other examples might be disclosure of the identities of covert CIA operatives[17] or disclosure that the government has secretly broken the enemy's code, thus alerting the enemy to change its cipher. In such situations, the harm from publication might be thought sufficiently likely, imminent, and serious to justify punishing the disclosure.

An important feature of these illustrations often passes unnoticed. What makes these examples so compelling is not only the nature and magnitude of the harm, but also the implicit assumption that the information does not meaningfully contribute to public debate. In most circumstances, there is no apparent value in having the public know the secret "sailing dates of transports" or the secret "location of troops" when there is no time for political action. Later, of course, such information may be critical in evaluating the effectiveness of our military leaders, but at the very moment the troops are set to attack it is unclear how publication of their location could meaningfully contribute to public discourse. The same may be said about the public disclosure that we have broken an enemy's code. My point is not that these illustrations involve low-value speech in the conventional sense of that term, but that they involve information that does not seem newsworthy at the moment of publication, and that this factor plays a significant role in making the illustrations persuasive.

The failure to notice this feature of these examples can lead to a serious failure of analysis. Indeed, just such a failure was implicit in the memorable hypothetical Justice Holmes first used to elucidate the clear and present danger test—the false cry of fire in a crowded theater.[18] Why can the false cry of fire be restricted? Because it creates a clear and present danger of a mad dash to the exits. Therefore, Holmes reasoned, the test for restricting speech is whether it creates a clear and present danger of serious harm. But the reasoning is spurious. Suppose the cry of fire is true? In that case, we would not punish the speech—even though it still causes a mad dash to the exits—because the value of the speech outweighs the harm it creates. Thus, at least two factors must be considered in analyzing this situation—the *harm* caused by the speech and the *value* of the speech.

Similarly, the reason for protecting the publication of the Pentagon Papers was not only that the disclosure would not "surely result in direct, immediate, and irreparable damage" to the nation, but also that the Pentagon Papers had serious value to informed public discourse. Suppose a newspaper accurately reports that American troops in Iraq recently murdered twenty insurgents in cold blood? As a result of this publication, insurgents quite predictably kidnap and murder twenty Americans. Can the newspaper constitutionally be punished for disclosing the initial massacre? I would argue "no." Even though there was a clear and present danger that the retaliation would follow, the information is simply too important to the American people for the government to punish its disclosure.

What this suggests is that to justify the criminal punishment of the press for publishing classified information, the government must prove that the publisher knew (a) it was publishing classified information; (b) the publication of which would result in likely, imminent, and serious harm to the national security; and (c) the publication of which would not meaningfully contribute to public debate. In practical effect, this has been the law of the United States for more than half a century, although there is no holding to this effect.[19]

Notes

1. Perhaps the closest the government ever came to such a prosecution involved a disclosure by the *Chicago Tribune* in 1942 that might have alerted the Japanese to the fact that the United States had broken their secret codes. See Lloyd Wendt, *Chicago Tribune: The Rise of a Great American Newspaper*, 627-636 (Rand McNally & Co., 1979).

2. 403 U.S. 713 (1971).

3. See Geoffrey R. Stone, *Perilous Times: Free Speech in Wartime from the Espionage Act of 1798 to the War on Terrorism*, 500-505 (W. W. Norton, 2004).

4. *United States v. New York Times Co.*, 328 F. Supp. 324, 325 (S.D. N.Y. 1971).

5. Id., at 727, 728, 730 (Stewart concurring). The government filed criminal charges against Ellsberg for leaking the Pentagon Papers, but the prosecution was abandoned as a result of prosecutorial misconduct. See Melville B. Nimmer, "National Security Secrets v. Free Speech: The Issues Left Undecided in the Ellsberg Case," 26 *Stan. L. Rev.* 311 (1974).

6. See *Brandenburg v. Ohio*, 395 U.S. 444, 447 (1969) (even express advocacy of unlawful conduct can be proscribed only if the advocacy "is directed to inciting or producing imminent lawless action and is likely to incite or produce such action"); *Kingsley International Pictures Corp. v. Regents of New York*, 360 U.S. 684, 689 (1959) (even "advocacy of conduct proscribed by law" in not "'a justification for denying free speech where the advocacy falls short of incitement and there is nothing to indicate that the advocacy would be immediately acted on'"); *Bridges v. California*, 314 U.S. 252, 273 (1941) (in order to punish expression, "the substantive evil must be extremely serious and the degree of imminence extremely high"); *Landmark Communications, Inc. v. Virginia*, 435 U.S. 829 (1978) (requiring not only clear and present danger, but also that the magnitude of the danger be serious). See also Kent Greenawalt, "'Clear and Present Danger' and Criminal Speech," in Lee C. Bollinger and Geoffrey R. Stone, *Eternally Vigilant: Free Speech in the Modern Era* 97, 119 (University of Chicago, 2002) (to punish speech, the evil must be: imminent, likely, and grave); Bernard Schwartz, "*Holmes v. Hand*: Clear and Present Danger or Advocacy of Unlawful Action?," 1994, *Sup. Ct. Rev.* 209, 240-241 ("the immediate law violation must be likely to occur").

7. Alexander Bickel, *The Morality of Consent*, 79-82 (Yale University Press, 1975).

8. This approach is not unique to the national security context. The Court has applied it to a broad range of issues involving the publication of confidential government information. See, e.g., *Florida Star v. B.J.F.*, 491 U.S. 524 (1989) (publication of rape victim's

name); *Smith v. Daily Mail Publishing Co.*, 443 U.S. 97 (1979) (publishing name of juvenile offender); *Landmark Communications, Inc. v. Virginia*, 435 U.S. 829 (1978) (publication of confidential matters before judicial review board); *Oklahoma Publishing Co. v. District Court*, 430 U.S. 308 (1977) (publishing name of juvenile offender); *Nebraska Press Association v. Stuart*, 427 U.S. 539 (1976) (publication of information about criminal defendant before trial); *Cox Broadcasting v. Cohn*, 420 U.S. 469 (1975) (publication of rape victim's name). In all of these decisions, the Court invoked the principle that although the government could prohibit public employees from disclosing the information in the first place, it could not thereafter enjoin or punish the media for further disseminating the information once it fell into the public domain.

9. A slightly different variant of this problem involves not unlawful disclosures by public employees, but some other underlying illegality. In *Bartnicki v. Vopper*, 532 U.S. 514 for example, Vopper, a radio talk show host was prosecuted for broadcasting a recording of a private telephone conversation. The recording had been made by a third person in violation of federal law. The third person had sent the tape to Vopper. Although the recording was unlawful, the Court held that Vopper could not constitutionally be held liable for damages for broadcasting it. The only decision in which the Supreme Court has held that a publisher could constitutionally be punished for distributing speech because the speech was produced or made available to the press as a result of an unlawful act involved child pornography. See *New York v. Ferber*, 458 U.S. 747 (1982). But the child pornography issue is readily distinguishable from all the other situations, including the disclosure of classified information by public employees, because the images presented in child pornography can easily be generated without engaging in actual child sexual abuse. See *Ashcroft v. The Free Speech Coalition*, 535 U.S. 234 (2002) (government cannot constitutionally punish the exhibition of images of children engaged in sex if they are produced by computer simulation or the use of body-double, rather than by actual child sexual abuses). In the classified information situation, the information made available to the public would not exist but for the underlying disclosure.

10. See 403 U.S., at 730 (Stewart, J. concurring); id., at 737 (White, J., concurring).

11. See Stephen Barnett, "The Puzzle of Prior Restraint," 29 *Stan. L. Rev.* 539, 551-553 (1977).

12. Paul Freund, "The Supreme Court and Civil Liberties," 4 *Vand. L. Rev.* 533, 539 (1951). See Martin Redish, "The Proper Role of the Prior Restraint Doctrine in First Amendment Theory," 70 *Va. L.* Rev. 53 (1984); William Mayton, "Toward a Theory of First Amendment Process: Injunctions of Speech, Subsequent Punishment, and the Costs of the Prior Restraint Doctrine," 67 *Cornell L. Rev.* 245 (1982); Stephen Barnett, "The Puzzle of Prior Restraint," 29 *Stan. L. Rev.* 539 (1977); Vincent Blasi, "Toward a Theory of Prior Restraint: The Central Linkage," 66 *Minn. L. Rev.* 11 (1981).

13. See, e.g., *Freedman v. Maryland*, 380 U.S. 51 (1965) (obscenity); *Near v. Minnesota*, 283 U.S. 697 (1931) (libel).

14. See David A. Strauss, "Freedom of Speech and the Common-Law Constitution," in Lee C. Bollinger and Geoffrey R. Stone, *Eternally Vigilant: Free Speech in the Modern Era*, 57-59 (University of Chicago Press, 2002) ("it is difficult to believe that the Court would have allowed newspaper editors to be punished, criminally, after they published the [Pentagon] Papers").

15. See *Landmark Communications, Inc. v. Virginia*, 435 U.S. 829 (1978); *Worrell Newspapers v. Westhafer*, 739 F.2d 1219, 1223 (7th Cir. 1984), aff'd 469 U.S. 1200 (1985).

16. *Near v. Minnesota*, 283 U.S. 697, 716 (1931).

17. See *Haig v. Agee*, 453 U.S. 280 (1981) (upholding the Secretary of State's revocation of a former CIA employee's passport for exposing the identities of covert CIA agents around the world).

18. *Schenck v. United States*, 249 U.S. 47, 52 (1919).

19. Requirement (c) may seem novel, but it is embedded in both First Amendment principle and First Amendment doctrine. Without some such requirement, no balance takes place and the First Amendment side of the equation is simply ignored. Without (c), the test would blithely assume that the harm of publication outweighs the value of publication. I should emphasize that (c) is not a requirement in considering the constitutionality of regulations of low-value speech, content-neutral regulations, content-based regulations that are not directed at particular ideas, items of information, or viewpoints, or even regulations directed at particular ideas, items of information, or viewpoints in special environments (such as public employment, schools, and government subsidy programs). But when the government attempts generally to restrict speech at the very core of the First Amendment, requirement (c) plays an important role in the analysis. The best illustration of the relevance of requirement (c) is in the evolution of the Court's doctrine in the area of speech causing unlawful conduct, where the Court requires both express incitement and clear and present danger. See Geoffrey R. Stone, "Dialogue," in Lee C. Bollinger and Geoffrey R. Stone, *Eternally Vigilant: Free Speech in the Modern Era*, 4-6 (University of Chicago Press, 2002); Bernard Schwartz, "*Holmes v. Hand*: Clear and Present Danger or Advocacy of Unlawful Action?," 1994, *Sup. Ct. Rev.* 209, 240-241; Gerald Gunther, "Learned Hand and the Origins of Modern First Amendment Doctrine: Some Fragments of History," 27 *Stan. L. Rev.* 719, 754, 755 (1975).

Journalists

IN what circumstances may the government criminally punish a journalist for receiving or soliciting classified documents or information from a government employee for the purpose of publication? This is a novel question. In all of American history, no journalist has *ever* been prosecuted under such a theory.

The First Amendment and the Criminal Law

The best place to begin is with ordinary criminal law principles. Such principles do not trump the Constitution, but they provide a touchstone for analysis. We can divide the most likely scenarios into three categories.

First, a journalist would violate ordinary criminal law principles if he knowingly coerces, bribes, or defrauds a public employee into disclosing classified information, if the employee could constitutionally be punished for disclosing that information.[1]

Second, a journalist would violate ordinary criminal law principles if he knowingly encourages, incites, persuades, or solicits a public employee to disclose classified information, if the employee could constitutionally be punished for disclosing that information.[2]

Third, a journalist would violate ordinary criminal law principles if he knowingly receives from a public employee (or, indeed, from any source) classified information that could not lawfully be disclosed by a public employee.[3]

Thus, a journalist who obtains classified information by bribery, solicitation, or passive receipt may be guilty of a crime, unless the First Amendment affords him its protection. Even though an act ordinarily is unlawful, it is not unlawful if it is protected by the First Amendment.

For example, the government can make it unlawful for any person to obstruct the draft. An individual who physically blocks access to a selective service office can be punished for doing so. But an individual who distributes leaflets criticizing the draft as immoral cannot constitutionally be punished, even though his ideas might persuade some people to refuse induction. The criminal law principle is the same, but the pamphleteer is protected by the First Amendment.[4]

Similarly, the government can make it a crime for any person to incite a breach of the peace. An individual who throws a chair in a bar can be punished for inciting a brawl. But an individual whose public speech triggers a fight ordinarily is protected by the First Amendment.[5] Put simply, that the government can make certain conduct unlawful does not mean it can punish that conduct when it is protected by the First Amendment.

The Problem of Incidental Impact

What does it mean to say that conduct is "protected by the First Amendment?" This is more complicated than one might expect, as there are many ways in which laws limit speech. First, a law may expressly restrict the communication of particular points of view, ideas, or items of information. For example, "No one may publicly criticize the war" or "No one may publish classified information." Because such laws may seriously distort the content of public debate and are often enacted for constitutionally questionable reasons, they are presumptively unconstitutional.[6]

Second, a law may expressly restrict communication, but *not* on the basis of content. For example, "No one may distribute leaflets in a public park" or "No one may erect a billboard near a public highway." Because such laws regulate speech, but not on the basis of content, they are analyzed through a process of balancing, in which the court determines whether the government interest outweighs the impact on speech.[7]

Third, a law may restrict what is essentially noncommunicative conduct, but in a way that has an incidental impact on speech. For example,

"No one may appear naked in public," as applied to an individual who marches naked on Main Street to protest antiobscenity laws, or "No one may engage in wiretapping," as applied to a reporter who wiretaps a congressman in the hope of hearing him accept a bribe. Because such laws do not expressly restrict speech, they are presumptively constitutional. A court will invalidate such laws only if the incidental effect on speech is substantial and substantially outweighs the government's interest in enforcing the law.[8]

In considering whether a law violates the First Amendment, it is necessary to determine which of these models applies. A law expressly prohibiting the press from publishing classified information clearly regulates content. Such a law would therefore be tested by the highest degree of First Amendment scrutiny.

But what of the laws we are dealing with here? In the first instance, we must look to the terms of the legislation.[9] If the government prosecutes a journalist for violating a law making it unlawful to encourage a public employee to disclose classified information for the purpose of publication, the law would seem to fall squarely within the first category. It regulates expression on the basis of content. Viewed in this light, the journalist presumably would be protected by the First Amendment to the same extent as the newspaper that publishes the information.

But it is not so simple. Suppose the journalist is prosecuted under a general law prohibiting any person to solicit the commission of a felony. This statute would apply to solicitation to commit murder, rape, arson, burglary, and fraud, as well as to unlawfully disclose classified information. It is not expressly directed at communicative crimes.[10] Hence, this would seem to fall into the third category. Like laws prohibiting public nudity and wiretapping, laws prohibiting solicitation to commit felonies have only an incidental effect on expression. Such a law is presumptively constitutional.

There are several ways out of this quandary. The simplest is for the government to prosecute those who bribe or solicit public employees to disclose classified information only under general laws prohibiting bribery and solicitation, rather than under laws expressly targeting communicative crimes. The laws currently on the books are all over the lot in this respect. Because my interest here is in the First Amendment rather than the statutory issues, I will assume we are dealing with prosecutions under general laws prohibiting bribery, solicitation, and the receipt of stolen property, which makes the problem more challenging.[11]

Let us assume, then, that a journalist is prosecuted for soliciting a public employee to reveal classified national security information, for which disclosure the employee could constitutionally be punished. Let us assume further that the journalist is prosecuted under a general criminal statute prohibiting any person to solicit another to commit a crime. As we have seen, if this law has only an incidental effect on speech, it will likely be constitutional, even as applied to a journalist.

But *why* should this be so? The answer is simple. Almost every law can have an incidental effect on speech. A law against public nudity (think of nude sunbathing) would prohibit public nudity by a person whose bare bottom is intended as a form of political protest. A law against speeding makes it more difficult for individuals to get to a demonstration or lecture on time. A law against open fires in public prohibits flag burning; a sales tax reduces the amount of money you have to support your favorite political causes; and a law against wiretapping makes it more difficult for reporters to gather news.[12]

The rationale of the incidental effects doctrine is largely one of practicality. Because almost every law can have some effect on speech, and because individuals would readily claim they were engaged in speech (even if they weren't) if that claim could make out a defense to a criminal charge ("I committed the robbery so I could give money to a political candidate"), an approach that required courts seriously to consider the incidental effects of laws on speech-related activities in *every* case would be a judicial nightmare.

Moreover, in almost all of these instances the individual has many other ways to achieve his goals. Instead of walking down Main Street naked, the protester can carry a sign criticizing antiobscenity laws. Instead of speeding to get to the lecture, the lecture-goer could have left on time. Instead of burning a flag in public, the war opponent can shred his flag and thus avoid the prohibition on open fires. In short, the *actual* impact of most laws having incidental effects on free expression is usually slight.

For these reasons, the Supreme Court has reasonably held that laws having only an incidental effect on free expression are presumptively constitutional and may be invalidated only in the very unusual situation in which they have a *substantial* impact on free expression.[13] This suggests that general laws prohibiting bribery and solicitation are not unconstitutional merely because they have an incidental effect on journalists who would like to bribe or solicit public employees to disclose classified information for the purpose of publication.

Incidental Impact as Applied to Reporters

Once again, however, it is not so simple. The incidental impact of these laws on the freedom of the press may be sufficiently serious to justify their invalidation. Certainly, some of the information that would be disclosed to the public as a result of unlawful disclosures would be of considerable value to the public. But the same would be true of unlawful journalistic wiretaps and burglaries. In some circumstances, journalists would be better able to discover valuable information if they could wiretap the offices of senators and burgle the homes of corporate executives. But I doubt we are about to hold wiretapping, trespass, and burglary laws unconstitutional as applied to journalists (though such a claim is not absurd). Because the seriousness of the incidental impact of laws against wiretapping and burglary is not much different from the seriousness of the incidental impact of laws against bribery and solicitation, the incidental impact of bribery and solicitation laws on freedom of the press would not seem sufficiently substantial to justify invalidating those laws as applied to journalists.

But we might not be dealing here with the conventional incidental-impact situation, in which the underlying crime is not inherently expressive. Speeding, being naked in public, wiretapping, burglary, making an open fire, and paying taxes are not inherently expressive acts. If the First Amendment is implicated in those situations, it is only because laws regulating those acts occasionally have an effect on expressive behavior. The effect on speech, in other words, is merely "incidental."

But in the public disclosure situation, the issue is more complex, because it involves two levels of conduct—the solicitation and the disclosure. Although a general law prohibiting solicitation to commit crimes has only an incidental effect on journalists who solicit public employees to disclose classified information, the crime solicited is itself a communicative act, and it is the *communication* that causes the harm. This is a subtle but important distinction.

In the burglary situation, for example, it is the invasion of the homeowner's property and privacy that causes the harm. It makes no difference to the criminal law whether the burglar is interested in stealing money, jewels, or information. That a journalist commits burglary in order to gather news rather than steal cash is irrelevant to the reason for prohibiting burglary. But if a journalist is punished for soliciting classified information from a public employee, the underlying act (the disclosure) is unlawful precisely because it involves expression. It is, indeed, the communication of the information that causes the harm that the government seeks to prevent. Thus, unlike the burglary situation, the bribery and solicitation situations are only quasi-incidental impact problems.

All this may seem needlessly abstruse and complex. But this is sometimes the nature of legal reasoning. General principles are useful to distinguish among different types of cases, but the principles are almost always imprecise at the margins. There are gradations. Sometimes it is best to ignore the gradations for the sake of simplicity, sometimes it is best to take the gradations into account. In this context, we are at the margin between laws that have only an incidental effect on expression and laws that regulate the content of expression. It would be simplistic to pretend that this is a routine case of mere incidental effect.[14]

Perhaps most important, it is essential to recall how we came to the conclusion that the government can constitutionally prohibit public employees from disclosing classified information to reporters for the purpose of publication. As we saw in chapter 1, that issue poses a potentially serious conflict between the First Amendment and the government's interests in efficiency and security. We allow the government to prohibit its employees from revealing information to the public not because the *harm* of disclosure necessarily outweighs the *value* of disclosure, but because public employees have consented to such a limitation of their rights and because it is useful for the government to have a clear and simple rule for its employees. Although that approach may be justified for internal management purposes, it substantially undervalues the potential importance of the disclosures to informed public debate.

Thus, as we saw in chapter 2, the government may not hold the press to the same standard it applies to its employees. For the same reason that the standard for government employees does not govern the press, it also should not govern the newsgathering activities of journalists.

In effect, newsgathering is an intermediate case. To resolve it, we must draw on two competing analogies: the government's authority to regulate the speech of its employees and the press's authority to publish information of value to the public.

Criminal Punishment and Newsgathering

At this point, it is necessary to return to the three ways in which journalists might obtain classified information from public employees: (1) bribery, coercion, or fraud; (2) solicitation, persuasion, or incitement; and (3) passive receipt. In the real world, of course, the lines blur, for the relationships between journalists and their sources are subtle and complex. Nonetheless, unless we embrace an all-or-nothing approach for the sake of simplicity, distinctions must be made.

Situations (3) and (1) are the easiest. Situation (3) is illustrated by the Pentagon Papers case, in which Daniel Ellsberg sent the classified documents unsolicited to Neil Sheehan of the *New York Times*. This situation is also illustrated by *Bartnicki v. Vopper*,[15] in which Vopper, a radio commentator, received in the mail from an anonymous source a tape recording of an unlawfully intercepted telephone conversation, which Vopper then played on the air. In both cases, the journalists passively received the information, though both knew or should have known that the information had been obtained and disclosed to them unlawfully.

Under traditional criminal law principles, both Sheehan and Vopper knowingly received "stolen" property. Nonetheless, because the information involved matters of public concern, both Sheehan and Vopper were protected by the First Amendment. As the Court explained in *Bartnicki*, when a journalist receives information "from a source who has obtained it unlawfully," the journalist may not be punished for the receipt or publication of the information, "absent a need of the highest order."[16]

In rejecting the argument that the government can punish journalists in order to deter those who unlawfully intercept conversations, the Court in *Bartnicki* reasoned that if "the sanctions that presently attach to [the unlawful acts] do not provide sufficient deterrence," then "perhaps those sanctions should be made more severe," but "it would be quite remarkable to hold" that a law-abiding journalist can constitutionally be punished merely for receiving and publishing that information "in order to deter conduct by a nonlaw-abiding third party."[17]

Thus, in the passive-receipt situation, where the journalist has not bribed or solicited the public employee to violate the law, neither the journalist nor the publisher can be criminally punished for receiving or possessing unlawfully disclosed information, the publication of which could not constitutionally be punished.

Situation (1) seems equally straightforward. The government has a legitimate interest in expecting its employees to obey the law. For a journalist to bribe, coerce, or defraud a public employee unlawfully to disclose classified national security information seems analogous to the wiretapping and burglary examples. Like wiretapping and burglary, bribery, coercion, and fraud are well-established crimes, far removed from the traditional processes of newsgathering. Although it might be "useful" for reporters to bribe and extort classified information from public employees, and although such conduct would sometimes result in the disclosure of valuable information, the government's legitimate interest in not having its employees bribed, coerced, or defrauded seems sufficiently weighty to justify the prohibition of such conduct.

Situation (2) is the trickiest. Like bribery, coercion, and fraud, solicitation is ordinarily unlawful. But that is also true of receiving stolen property and, as we have seen, that an act is ordinarily unlawful is not conclusive in the face of the First Amendment. Although it would be easy to envision a legal regime in which journalists were prohibited from encouraging public employees to reveal classified information, such a regime would disregard the need to strike a proper balance between government secrecy and an informed public.

Just as we grant the government "too much" authority to protect secrecy at its source, so, too, must we grant the press "too much" authority to probe that secrecy. To make it a crime for journalists to attempt to persuade public employees to disclose classified information that might contribute to public debate would place too much weight on the secrecy side of the scale. The standard that defines the government's power to punish its employees for disclosing classified information ("potential harm to the national security") was not designed to determine the balance between government secrecy and freedom of the press.

Indeed, building upon the Court's reasoning in *Bartnicki*, it would seem that the appropriate government response to such solicitations is not to prosecute journalists, but to increase the penalties for government employees who violate the law. Moreover, an effort to apply the crime of solicitation to the myriad interactions between journalists and their sources would prove just as messy as an effort to regulate more precisely the relationship between the government and its employees. Because it is often difficult to define when a conversation passes the line between a discussion of policy and a solicitation to crime, the enforcement of solicitation law in this setting would be uncertain, confusing and treacherous. The interjection of the government into the very heart of the journalist-source relationship could have a serious chilling effect on journalist-source exchanges.

One way to address these concerns (indeed, probably a constitutional requirement), would be to limit the crime of solicitation in this context to *express incitement* of unlawful conduct (e.g., "give me the classified document, the disclosure of which is unlawful"). But as First Amendment history and doctrine teach, even a requirement of express incitement is an inadequate safeguard. The Court has held (at least in the context of public speech) that even express incitement of unlawful conduct cannot constitutionally be proscribed, unless it creates a likely and imminent danger of serious harm.[18]

The most sensible course is to hold that the government cannot constitutionally punish journalists for encouraging public employees to unlawfully disclose classified information, unless the journalist (a) expressly incites the employee to unlawfully disclose classified information, (b) knows that publication of this information would likely cause imminent and grave harm to the national security, and (c) knows that publication of the information would not meaningfully contribute to public debate.

It is important to keep in mind that the government is not powerless in this situation. As in *Bartnicki*, the government's primary means for protecting its legitimate interests is by punishing its employees for disclosing classified information. The United States has made it through more than two hundred years without ever finding it necessary to prosecute a journalist for soliciting a public employee to disclose confidential national security information. This is not because such solicitations have never occurred, but because employees have usually complied with the law and, when they haven't, the press has either acted responsibly or the resulting harm has not been thought sufficiently serious to justify such an intrusion into the freedom of the press.[19]

Who Is a Journalist?

This still leaves a vexing question. Who is a journalist? Surely, reporters for the *Washington Post* or CNN qualify. But what about a professor writing a book, a blogger, the editor of a school newspaper, a lobbyist, or a spy?[20] The idea of courts deciding as a matter of constitutional interpretation who is and is not a member of the "press" for First Amendment purposes is daunting, at best.

Indeed, the Supreme Court acknowledged this in *Branzburg v. Hayes*,[21] in which the Court declined to recognize a robust First Amendment-based journalist-source privilege, in part because recognition of such a privilege would make it "necessary to define those categories of newsmen who qualified for the privilege, a questionable procedure in light of the traditional doctrine that liberty of the press is the right of the lonely pamphleteer . . . just as much as of the large metropolitan publisher."[22]

This sort of problem arises whenever anyone challenges a law because of its incidental effect on speech. This is one reason why the Court is reluctant to invalidate laws on that basis. Despite this difficulty, however, the Court has invalidated laws on this premise when the law's impact on free expression is sufficiently severe. In *NAACP v. Alabama*,[23] for example, the Court held that Alabama could not constitutionally require the NAACP to disclose its membership lists. The Court explained that the disclosure of such information in Alabama at the height of the civil rights movement might "induce members to withdraw from the Association and dissuade others from joining it because of fear of exposure of their beliefs."[24] The Court therefore held the law unconstitutional as applied to the NAACP, opening the door to similar challenges to other laws by other individuals and organizations.[25]

Similarly, in *Boy Scouts of America v. Dale*,[26] the Court invalidated a state antidiscrimination law as applied to the Boy Scouts. The Court held that for the state to require the Boy Scouts to allow gay scoutmasters would seriously impair the group's right of "expressive association." This decision, too, opened the door to challenges by other groups to other laws and regulations. Although the question "who is the press?" is not identical to the questions "what organizations are like the NAACP?" or "what organizations are like the Boy Scouts?," the nature of the inquiries is the same.

In effect, we have three alternatives. First, rather than decide who is a member of the press, we could conclude that the best course is to protect anyone who solicits classified information from public employees. This would extend First Amendment protection to some individuals who are not engaged in First Amendment activity. The primary justification for this approach would be that it avoids the need to decide who is a member of the "press." This is not as peculiar as it might seem, for in this context, unlike most incidental restriction situations, a very high percentage of those who engage in the activity (soliciting classified information from public employees) are likely to be journalists. Thus, the overinclusiveness of this approach would be relatively small.

Second, we could treat journalists as if they are not journalists. That is, to avoid having to decide who is a member of the "press," we could hold that even members of the press can be punished for the receipt or solicitation of classified information. In light of the analysis up to this point, however, this approach seems too drastic. Ironically, it would seriously undermine the freedom of the press in order to avoid deciding who is entitled to the freedom of the press.

Though ironic, this judgment would not be unprecedented. To the contrary, as already noted, this was part of the Court's reasoning in *Branzburg* with respect to the journalist-source privilege. But *Branzburg* is distinguishable. In *Branzburg*, the Court concluded that a journalist-source privilege was unnecessary. Whatever the merits of that conclusion, the idea that the government could criminally punish reporters merely for receiving or requesting classified information (even though the press has a First Amendment right to publish that information), in order to avoid deciding who is a journalist, seems perverse.

Third, we could bite the bullet and decide, as a matter of First Amendment interpretation, who is and is not a member of the "press." This might not be quite as difficult as it seems, or at least as difficult as the Court thought at the time of *Branzburg*. In the years since that decision, forty-nine states and the District of Columbia have adopted some form of journalist-source privilege, all of which require courts to answer the question, "Who is a journalist?"[27] Courts therefore have plenty of experience with this issue. Of course, deciding this as a constitutional matter is different from deciding it as a matter of statutory or common law interpretation.[28] The most straightforward definition would be a functional one. That is, a member of the "press" for these purposes is a person who seeks information for the purpose of disseminating it to the public. This inquiry seems both manageable and preferable to the alternatives.[29]

But what about spies? What is to prevent an enemy spy from creating a blog, soliciting classified information from public employees, and then insulating herself from criminal punishment by publishing the classified information on her blog, rather than transmitting it secretly to the enemy? One answer, of course, is that in many instances this tactic would significantly dilute the value of the spy's work. Often, espionage is most valuable when the nation spied upon does not know that its secrets are not secret.

But there is a more fundamental answer. This sort of issue arises throughout First Amendment law. Is a person who criticizes the war in Iraq attempting to weaken our national resolve in order to aid the enemy, or is he participating constructively in public debate? Is he a traitor, or a patriot? The words he uses and the "harm" he causes may be precisely the same, regardless of his motive. In the evolution of First Amendment jurisprudence, we learned long ago that inquiries into subjective intent and personal motivation are usually fruitless—and often dangerous—in the context of free speech. In deciding whether an individual may be punished for her speech, it is necessary to focus on what she says and on the danger she creates, rather than on her motives. Even a traitor or a spy can meaningfully contribute to public debate, despite her bad motivations.[30]

Notes

1. Getting an employee drunk would also fall into this category.

2. This category includes the crimes of conspiracy and attempt. On the crime of solicitation, see Wayne R. LaFave, Criminal Law § 11.1 (West Pub. Co. 4th ed., 2002); Model Penal Code § 5.02; Kent Greenawalt, "Clear and Present Danger and Criminal Speech," in

Lee C. Bollinger and Geoffrey R. Stone, *Eternally Vigilant: Free Speech in the Modern Era*, 113-119 (University of Chicago, 2002).

3. This is merely an application of the traditional crime of receiving stolen property. There are subtleties in the meaning of "stolen" as applied to information, as distinct from documents, but the basic principle of the traditional criminal law concept would clearly apply to information as well as objects in situations like the one under consideration. It is a defense to the crime that the recipient intends to return the property (or information) to its lawful owner without in any way using it. Thus, a reporter who receives such a document and immediately returns it to the government and never discloses it or its contents to anyone else would not be guilty of a crime. On the crime of receipt of stolen property, see LaFave, Criminal Law at § 20.2 (cited in note 53); Model Penal Code § 223.6.

4. In the early years of First Amendment doctrine, the Supreme Court upheld convictions in such circumstances. See *Schenck v. United States*, 249 U.S. 47 (1919); *Debs v. United States*, 249 U.S. 211 (1919). Over time, however, the Court embraced a much more speech-protective approach. See *Brandenburg v. Ohio*, 395 U.S. 444 (1969). See generally Gerald Gunther, "Learned Hand and the Origins of Modern First Amendment Doctrine: Some Fragments of History," 27 *Stan. L. Rev.* 719 (1975); Herman Schwartz, "*Holmes v. Hand*: Clear and Present Danger or Advocacy of Unlawful Action?," 1994, *Sup. Ct. Rev.* 209; Frank Strong, "Fifty Years of 'Clear and Present Danger': From *Schenck* to *Brandenburg*—and Beyond," 1969, *Sup. Ct. Rev.* 41.

5. See *Brandenburg v. Ohio*, 395 U.S. 444 (1969). Whether there are any circumstances in which the speaker can be punished for causing a riot is unclear. In *Feiner v. New York*, 340 U.S. 315 (1951), the Court upheld such a conviction where the speaker "undertook incitement to riot." Subsequent decisions have been much more protective of speakers, however. See, e.g., *Edwards v. South Carolina*, 372 U.S. 229 (1963) (reversing convictions); *Cox v. Louisiana*, 379 U.S. 536 (1965) (reversing convictions).

6. As we saw in chapter 1, in the public employment situation such regulations may not be presumptively unconstitutional. On content-based restrictions of speech, see Elena Kagan, "Private Speech, Public Purpose: The Role of Governmental Motive in First Amendment Doctrine," 63 *U. Chi. L. Rev.* 413, 494-508 (1996); Susan Williams, "Content Discrimination and the First Amendment," 139 *U. Pa. L. Rev.* 615 (1991); Geoffrey R. Stone, "Content Regulation and the First Amendment," 25 *Wm. & Mary L. Rev.* 189 (1983); Paul Stephan, "The First Amendment and Content Discrimination," 68 *Va. L. Rev.* 203 (1982). As noted, laws regulating low value speech on the basis of content involve a separate analysis under the First Amendment.

7. See Geoffrey R. Stone, "Content-Neutral Restrictions," 54 *U. Chi. L. Rev.* 46 (1987).

8. On "incidental" restrictions, see Jed Rubenfeld, "The First Amendment's Purpose," 53 *Stan. L. Rev.* 767, 769 (2001) (arguing that "there is no such thing as a free speech immunity based on the claim that someone wants to break an otherwise constitutional law for First Amendment purposes"); Elena Kagan, "Private Speech, Public Purpose: The Role of Governmental Motive in First Amendment Doctrine," 63 *U. Chi. L. Rev.* 413, 494-508 (1996) (arguing that the distinction between direct and incidental restrictions in First Amendment analysis can be explained largely in terms of the concern with avoiding possible improper governmental motivation); Michael Dorf, "Incidental Burdens on Fundamental Rights," 109 *Harv. L. Rev.* 1175 (1996) (arguing that although "sound reasons can be advanced for taking direct burdens more seriously than incidental burdens," this does

not mean "that incidental burdens should never count as constitutional infringements"); Geoffrey R. Stone, "Content-Neutral Restrictions," 54 *U. Chi. L. Rev.* 46, 114 (1987) (arguing that although "the general presumption is that incidental restrictions do not raise a question of First Amendment review," courts will invalidate such restrictions if they have "a highly disproportionate impact" or particular viewpoints or "significantly limit the opportunities for free expression"). For illustrative decisions upholding laws having an incidental impact on speech, see *Barnes v. Glen Theatre, Inc.*, 501 U.S. 560 (1991) (nude dancing); *Arcara v. Cloud Books*, 478 U.S. 697 (1986) (closing building used for prostitution, as applied to "adult" bookstore); *United States v. O'Brien*, 391 U.S. 367 (1968) (draftcard burning). In a few decisions, the Court has held incidental restrictions unconstitutional. See *Boy Scouts of America v. Dale*, 530 U.S. 640 (2000) (antidiscrimination law); *Brown v. Socialist Workers '74 Campaign Committee*, 459 U.S. 87 (1982) (disclosure of campaign contributions); *NAACP v. Alabama*, 357 U.S. 449 (1958) (disclosure of NAACP membership lists).

9. The most comprehensive source on the relevant laws is Harold Edgar and Benno Schmidt, Jr., "The Espionage Statutes and Publication of Defense Information," 73 *Colum. L. Rev.* 929 (1973).

10. Of course, solicitation, like bribery and conspiracy, involves the use of words. But, at least in the context of private (as opposed to public) speech, such language is assumed to have the quality of an "act" and does not itself raise a serious First Amendment issue. See Frederick Schauer, "'Private' Speech and the 'Private' Forum: *Givhan v. Western Line School District*," 1979, *Sup. Ct. Rev.* 217.

11. For examples of the relevant laws, see 18 U.S.C. §§ 793 et seq.; 50 U.S.C. § 421 et seq.

12. See *Cohen v. Cowles Media Co.*, 501 U.S. 663 (1991) (no First Amendment press exemption from breach of contract law); *Zurcher v. Stanford Daily*, 436 U.S. 547 (1978) (no First Amendment press exemption from newsroom searches); *Branzburg v. Hayes*, 408 U.S. 665 (1972) (no First Amendment-based journalist-source privilege); *Associated Press v. NLRB*, 301 U.S. 103 (1937) (no First Amendment press exemption to NLRA).

13. For examples of decisions invalidating laws on this basis, see *Boy Scouts of America v. Dale*, 530 U.S. 640 (2000) (antidiscrimination law); *Brown v. Socialist Workers '74 Campaign Committee*, 459 U.S. 87 (1982) (disclosure of campaign contributions); *NAACP v. Alabama*, 357 U.S. 449 (1958) (disclosure of NAACP membership lists).

14. Another example of this sort of problem involves prosecutions of speakers under breach of the peace statutes. Such laws ordinarily do not specify any particular content for restriction. Rather, they prohibit any conduct that causes (or knowingly or intentionally causes) a breach of the peace. It matters not under the statute whether the conduct is speech or nonspeech or whether the speech carries any particular message. Viewed from this perspective, such laws might be thought to have only an incidental effect on expression. In fact, however, the Supreme Court has always treated such laws as content-based restrictions of speech whenever the conduct prosecuted is speech and the breach of the peace was caused by the content of the speech. Put differently, a law is analyzed as content-based, regardless of how it is drafted, whenever its application turns on the communicative impact of speech. See, e.g., *Edwards v. South Carolina*, 372 U.S. 229 (1963); *Terminiello v. Chicago*, 337 U.S. 1 (1949); *Cantwell v. Connecticut*, 310 U.S. 296 (1940). See also John Hart Ely, *Democracy and Distrust*, 111 (Harvard, 1980) (a law is content-based when it turns in application "on how

people will react to what the speaker is saying"); Jed Rubenfeld, "The First Amendment's Purpose," 53 *Stan. L. Rev.* 767, 777 (2001); Geoffrey R. Stone, "Content Regulation and the First Amendment," 25 *Wm. & Mary L. Rev.* 189, 207-217 (1983).

15. 532 U.S. 514 (2001).

16. 532 U.S., at 528.

17. Id. at 530.

18. See *Brandenburg v. Ohio*, 395 U.S. 444 (1969) (even express advocacy of violence cannot be proscribed consistent with the First Amendment unless it constitutes "incitement to imminent lawless action" and action is likely to occur imminently).

19. Another possibility is that public officials are loathe to prosecute the press because they are reluctant to trigger widespread press criticism.

20. *United States v. Rosen*, 445 F. Supp. 2d 602 (E.D. Va. 2006), involved a prosecution of two lobbyists, employed by the American Israel Public Affairs Committee. The defendants allegedly obtained classified information from an employee of the Department of Defense, which they then allegedly transmitted to members of the media, foreign policy analysts, and officials of a foreign government. The public employee pled guilty of violating 18 U.S.C. §§ 793(d) and (g), 50 U.S.C. §783 and 18 U.S.C. § 371. The defendants were charged with violating 18 U.S.C. § 793(g), which prohibits any person to conspire to transmit classified information to any person not entitled to receive it. The district court rejected the defendants' motion to dismiss the indictment on the ground that it violates the First Amendment. The district court properly recognized that collecting and publishing information about the national security "is at the core of the First Amendment's guarantees," that "the mere invocation of 'national security' or 'government secrecy' does not foreclose a First Amendment inquiry," and that the First Amendment provides less protection to public employees than to those who do not "have access to the information by virtue of their official position." The district court then went off-track, however, in holding that *New York Times v. United States* is limited to prior restraints and, astonishingly, that lobbyists (and presumably even journalists) may constitutionally be punished for knowingly disseminating information that is "potentially harmful" to the national security. The district court cited no precedents to support this conclusion, which flies in the face of at least fifty years of Supreme Court jurisprudence. The district court correctly treated 18 U.S.C. § 793(g) as a content-based restriction of potentially important speech, but then ignored its own admonition that the First Amendment treats nonpublic employees quite differently than public employees. In practical effect, the court applied the standard it had carefully enunciated for the former to the latter. In this respect, the decision seems clearly erroneous. Even if *New York Times* is limited to prior restraints, the standard in this context at the very least must embody an element of "clear and present danger."

21. 408 U.S. 665 (1972).

22. Id. at 704.

23. 357 U.S. 449 (1958).

24. Id. at 463.

25. See, e.g., *Brown v. Socialist Workers '74 Campaign Committee*, 459 U.S. 87 (1982) (invalidating the provisions of a state campaign reporting law as applied to the Socialist Workers Party, "a minor political party which historically has been the object of harassment").

26. 530 U.S. 640 (2000).

27. See Geoffrey R. Stone, "Why We Need a Federal Reporter's Privilege," 34 *Hofstra L. Rev.* 39, 42 n.12 (2005) and chapter 4.

28. See id., at 47-48. Similar issues arise with respect to the priest-penitent privilege. Deciding who is protected by the priest-penitent privilege raises potentially thorny First Amendment concerns, but courts have done it for centuries. See Ronald J. Colombo, "Forgive Us Our Sins: The Inadequacies of the Clergy-Penitent Privilege," 73 *N.Y.U. L. Rev.* 225 (1998). In that context, courts have usually taken a functional approach to the inquiry. See, e.g., *In re Grand Jury Investigation*, 918 F.2d 374, 377 (3d Cir. 1990); *In re Verplank*, 329 F. Supp. 433 (C.D. Cal. 1971); *Eckmann v. Board of Education of Hawthorn School District No. 17*, 106 F.R.D. 70 (E.D. Mo. 1985).

29. See *In re Madden*, 151 F.3d 125, 130 (3d Cir. 1998); *von Bulow v. von Bulow*, 811 F.2d 136, 143-144 (2d Cir. 1987).

30. See Geoffrey R. Stone, *Perilous Times: Free Speech in Wartime from the Espionage Act of 1798 to the War on Terrorism*, 217-220. On the other hand, there are many circumstances in which the law regulates individuals who are "agents" of a foreign power. The criminal punishment of such individuals for soliciting classified information from public employees with the intent of harming the United States might well be a permissible accommodation to the legitimate needs of the nation. Certainly, the mere pretext of being a journalist need not insulate such individuals from prosecution. See Harold Edgar and Benno Schmidt, Jr., "Curtiss-Wright Comes Home: Executive Power and National Security Secrecy," 21 *Harv. C.R.-C.L. L. Rev.* 349, 354 (1986) ("publication and espionage should not be encompassed within a single prohibition, except in those rare instances where the type of information at issue is extremely sensitive and of little value to informed public debate").

The Journalist-Source Privilege

IN what circumstances can the government compel a journalist to reveal the identity of a public employee or other individual who disclosed classified information to the journalist to enable him to publish it?

The Nature of Privileges

The goal of most legal privileges is to promote open communication in circumstances in which society wants to encourage such communication. There are many such privileges, including the attorney-client privilege,[1] the doctor-patient privilege,[2] the psychotherapist-patient privilege,[3] the privilege for confidential spousal communications,[4] and the priest-penitent privilege.[5]

In each of these instances, three judgments implicitly support recognition of the privilege: (1) the relationship is one in which open communication is important to society; (2) in the absence of a privilege, such communication will be inhibited; and (3) the cost to the legal system of losing access to the privileged information is outweighed by the benefit to society of open communication in the protected relationship.

Consider, for example, the psychotherapist-patient privilege. If patients know that their psychotherapists could routinely disclose or be compelled to disclose their confidential communications made for the purpose of treatment, they would naturally be more reluctant to reveal intimate or embarrassing facts about their experiences, thoughts, and beliefs. But without those revelations, psychotherapists would be hindered in their ability to offer appropriate advice and treatment to their patients. To facilitate treatment, we might create a privilege that prohibits psychotherapists from disclosing confidential matters revealed to them by a patient, unless the patient elects to waive the privilege.

Suppose, for example, Patient tells Psychotherapist that he was sexually abused by Teacher several years earlier. Teacher is now under investigation for sexual abuse of his students, and Psychotherapist is called to testify before the grand jury. Psychotherapist is asked, "Did Patient tell you he had been sexually abused by Teacher?" If a psychotherapist-patient privilege exists in the jurisdiction, Psychotherapist will be barred from answering the question without Patient's permission. The effect of the privilege is to deprive the investigation of relevant evidence in order to promote open communication in the treatment setting.

At this point, it is important to note a critical feature of privileges. If Patient would not have disclosed this information to Psychotherapist in the absence of a psychotherapist-patient privilege, then the criminal investigation loses *nothing* because of the privilege. This is so because, without the privilege, Psychotherapist would not have learned about Teacher's abuse of Patient in the first place. In that circumstance, the privilege creates the best of all possible outcomes: it promotes effective treatment at no cost to the legal system.

Of course, it is not that simple. It is impossible to measure precisely the cost of privileges to the legal process. If Patient would have revealed the information to Psychotherapist *even without the privilege*, then the privilege imposes a cost because it shields from disclosure a communication that would have been made even in the absence of a privilege. The ideal rule would privilege only those communications that would not have been made without the privilege.

This highlights another important feature of privileges: the privilege "belongs" to the person whose communication society wants to encourage (i.e., the client or patient), not to the attorney or doctor.[6] If the client or patient is indifferent to the confidentiality of the communication at the time it is made, or elects to waive the privilege at any time, the attorney or doctor has no authority to assert the privilege.[7] The attorney or doctor is merely the agent of the client or patient.[8]

The Journalist-Source Privilege

The logic of the journalist-source privilege is similar to that described above. Public policy supports the idea that individuals who possess information of significant value to the public ordinarily should be encouraged to convey that information to the public. We acknowledge and act upon this policy in many ways, including, for example, by providing copyright protection.[9]

Sometimes, though, individuals who possess such information are reluctant to have it known that they are the source. They may fear retaliation, gaining a reputation as a "snitch," losing their privacy, or simply getting "involved." A congressional staffer, for example, may have reason to believe that a senator has taken a bribe. She may want someone to investigate, but may not want to get personally involved. Or, an employee of a corporation may know that his employer is manufacturing an unsafe product, but may not want coworkers to know he was the source of the leak.

In such circumstances, individuals may refuse to disclose the information unless they have some way to protect their confidentiality. In our society, often the best way to reveal such information is through the press. But without a journalist-source privilege, such sources may decide silence is the better part of wisdom.

A journalist-source privilege thus makes sense for the same reason as the attorney-client privilege, the doctor-patient privilege, and the psychotherapist-patient privilege. It is in society's interest to encourage the communication, and without a privilege the communication will often be chilled. Moreover, in many instances the privilege will impose no cost on the legal system, because without the privilege the source might not disclose the information. Consider the congressional staffer example. Without a privilege, the staffer might never report the bribe and the crime will remain undetected. With the privilege, the source will speak with the journalist, who will publish the story, leading to an investigation that might uncover the bribe. In this situation, law enforcement is actually better with the privilege than without it, and this puts to one side the benefit to society of learning of the alleged bribe independent of any criminal investigation.

For this reason, forty-nine states and the District of Columbia recognize some version of the journalist-source privilege either by statute or common law.[10] It is long past time for the federal government to enact such a privilege as well. There is no sensible reason for the federal system not to recognize a journalist-source privilege to deal with situations like the congressional staffer and the corporate employee. In these circumstances, the absence of a journalist-source privilege *harms* the public interest. There are, of course, more difficult cases, and I will return to them later. But some form of journalist-source privilege is essential to foster the fundamental value of an informed citizenry.

Moreover, the absence of a federal privilege creates an intolerable situation for both journalists and sources. Consider a reporter who works in New York whose source is willing to tell her about an unsafe product, but only if the reporter promises him confidentiality. New York has a shield law, but the federal government does not. If the disclosure results in litigation or prosecution in the state courts of New York, the reporter can protect the source, but if the litigation or prosecution is in federal court, the reporter cannot invoke the privilege. This generates uncertainty, and uncertainty breeds silence. The absence of a federal privilege directly undermines the policies of forty-nine states and the District of Columbia and wreaks havoc on the legitimate and good-faith understandings and expectations of sources and reporters throughout the nation. This is an unnecessary and, indeed, irresponsible state of affairs.

The Journalist-Source Privilege and the First Amendment

One response to the call for federal legislation is that such a law is unnecessary because the First Amendment should solve the problem. This is wrong at many levels.[11] Most obviously, constitutional law sets a minimum baseline for the protection of individual liberties. It does not define the ceiling of such liberties.[12] That a particular practice or policy does not violate the Constitution does not mean it is good policy. This is evident in an endless list of laws that go far beyond constitutional requirements in supporting individual rights, ranging from the Civil Rights Act of 1964,[13] to legislative restrictions on certain surveillance practices,[14] to tax exemptions for religious organizations,[15] to regulations of the electoral process.[16]

Moreover, the journalist-source privilege poses not only a question of individual liberties, but also an important public policy issue about how best to support and strengthen the marketplace of ideas. Just as the nonconstitutional attorney-client privilege is about promoting a healthy legal system,[17] the nonconstitutional journalist-source privilege is about fostering a healthy political system.

Returning to the First Amendment, in 1972 the Supreme Court, in *Branzburg v. Hayes*,[18] addressed the question of whether the First Amendment embodies a journalist-source privilege.[19] The four dissenting justices concluded that "when a reporter is asked to appear before a grand jury and reveal confidences," the government should be required to:

(1) show that there is probable cause to believe that the newsman has information that is clearly relevant to a specific probable violation of law; (2) demonstrate that the information sought cannot be obtained by alternative means less destructive of First Amendment rights; and (3) demonstrate a compelling and overriding interest in the information.[20]

The opinion of the Court, however, rejected this conclusion and held that, as long as an investigation is conducted in good faith and not for the purpose of disrupting "a reporter's relationship with his news sources," the First Amendment does not protect either the source or the reporter from having to disclose relevant information to a grand jury.[21]

If this were all there were to *Branzburg*, it clearly would seem to have settled the First Amendment issue. But Justice Powell did something quite puzzling, for he not only joined the opinion of the Court, but also filed a separate concurring opinion that seemed directly at odds with the Court's opinion.[22] Specifically, Powell stated that in each case the "asserted claim to privilege should be judged on its facts by the striking of a proper balance between freedom of the press and the obligation of all citizens to give relevant testimony with respect to criminal conduct."[23]

Thus, Justice Powell seemed to embrace an approach between that of the four justices in dissent and the four other justices in the majority. Had he not joined the majority opinion, his concurring opinion, as the "swing" opinion, would clearly have stated the "law," even though no other justice agreed with him. But because he joined the opinion of the Court, no one has ever been quite sure what to make of his position. The result has been chaos in the lower federal courts about the extent to which the First Amendment embodies a journalist-source privilege.[24] Is there essentially no privilege, as suggested in the majority opinion, or is Powell's balancing approach the constitutional test? For more than thirty years, the Court has allowed this confusion to percolate in the lower federal courts.

This is another reason why a federal statute is necessary. We have lived too long with this uncertainty. The current state of affairs leaves sources, journalists, prosecutors, and lower federal courts without any clear guidance, and the scope of the First Amendment-based journalist-source privilege differs significantly from one part of the nation to another.[25] A federal law recognizing a journalist-source privilege would eliminate this confusion and offer much-needed guidance about the degree of confidentiality participants in the federal system may and may not expect. Especially in situations like these, where individuals are making difficult decisions about whether to put themselves at risk by revealing information of significant value to the public, clear rules are *essential*.

This brings me back to the relationship between constitutional law and federal legislation. If a robust journalist-source privilege is not required by the First Amendment, why (apart from considerations of uniformity) should Congress enact a privilege that goes beyond whatever the Court held in *Branzburg*? Beyond the point made earlier that the Constitution does not exhaust sound public policy, the Court in *Branzburg* relied heavily on two important First Amendment doctrines to justify its decision, neither of which is relevant to the issue of federal legislation.[26] Indeed, that is why, despite *Branzburg*, forty-nine states and the District of Columbia have felt comfortable recognizing some form of the journalist-source privilege.

First, as we have seen in chapter 3, as a general matter of First Amendment interpretation, the Court is reluctant to invalidate a law merely because it has an *incidental* effect on First Amendment freedoms.[27] Laws that *directly* regulate expression (e.g., "No one may criticize the government" or "No one may distribute leaflets at the Mall") are the central concern of the First Amendment.[28] Laws that only incidentally affect free expression (e.g., a speed limit applied to someone who speeds to get to a demonstration or to express his opposition to speed limits) will almost never violate the First Amendment.[29] Except in highly unusual circumstances, in which the application of such a law would have a substantial effect on First Amendment freedoms,[30] the Court routinely rejects such First Amendment challenges.[31]

The reason for this doctrine is not that such laws cannot dampen free expression, but that the implementation of a constitutional doctrine that allowed *every* law to be challenged whenever it impinges even indirectly on someone's freedom of expression would be a judicial nightmare. Does an individual have a First Amendment right not to pay taxes, because taxes reduce the amount of money she has available to support political causes? Does an individual have a First Amendment right to violate a law against public urination, because he wants to urinate on a public building to express his hostility to government policy? Does a reporter have a First Amendment right to violate laws against burglary or wiretapping, because burglary and wiretapping will enable him to get an important story?

To avoid such ad hoc line-drawing, the Court simply *presumes* that laws of general application are constitutional, even as applied to speakers and journalists, except in extraordinary circumstances.[32] Predictably, the Court invoked this principle in *Branzburg*: "[T]he First Amendment does not invalidate every incidental burdening of the press that may result from the enforcement of civil or criminal statutes of general applicability."[33]

This is a sound basis for the Court to be wary of constitutionalizing a strong journalist-source privilege, but it has no weight in the *legislative* context. Courts necessarily proceed on the basis of precedent, and they are quite sensitive to the dangers of "slippery slopes." Legislation, however, properly considers problems "one step at a time" and legislators need not reconcile each law with every other law in order to meet their responsibilities.

For the Court to recognize a journalist-source privilege but not, for example, a privilege of journalists to commit burglary or wiretapping, would pose a serious challenge to the judicial process. But for Congress to address the privilege issue without fretting over journalistic burglary or wiretapping is simply not a problem. This is a fundamental difference between the judicial and legislative processes.

Second, recognition of a journalist-source privilege necessarily requires someone to determine who, exactly, is a "journalist." As we saw in chapter 3, for the Court to decide this question *as a matter of First Amendment interpretation* would fly in the face of more than two hundred years of constitutional wisdom. The idea of defining or "licensing" the press in this manner is anathema to our constitutional traditions. The Court has never gone down this road, and with good reason. As the Court observed in *Branzburg*, if the Court recognized a First Amendment privilege "it would be necessary to define those categories of newsmen who qualified for the privilege, a questionable procedure in light of the traditional doctrine that liberty of the press is the right of the lonely pamphleteer . . . just as much as of the large metropolitan publisher. . . ."[34]

Although this was a serious constraint on the Court in *Branzburg*, it poses a much more manageable issue in the context of legislation. Government often treats different speakers and publishers differently from one another. Which reporters are allowed to attend a White House press briefing? Which are eligible to be embedded with the military? Broadcasting is regulated,[35] but print journalism is not. Legislation treats the cable medium differently from both broadcasting and print journalism. These categories need not conform perfectly to the undefined phrase "the press" in the First Amendment. Differentiation among different elements of the media is constitutional, as long as it is not based on viewpoint or any other invidious consideration, and as long as the differentiation is reasonable.[36] Whereas the Court is wisely reluctant to define "the press" for purposes of the First Amendment, it will grant Congress considerable deference in deciding who, as a matter of sound public policy, should be covered by the journalist-source privilege.

Thus, the primary reasons relied upon by the Court in *Branzburg* for its reluctance to recognize a robust First Amendment journalist-source privilege do not stand in the way of legislation to address the issue. To the contrary, the very weaknesses of the judicial process that make it difficult for a court to address this problem as a constitutional matter are precisely the strengths of Congress to address it well as a legislative matter.

The Costs of a Journalist-Source Privilege

The primary argument against *any* privilege is that it deprives the judicial or other investigative process of relevant evidence. Of course, there is nothing novel about that. Almost all rules of evidence deprive the fact-finder of relevant evidence. This is true not only of privileges, but also of rules against hearsay and opinion evidence, rules excluding proof of repairs and compromises, the exclusionary rule, the privilege against compelled self-incrimination, and rules protecting trade secrets and the identity of confidential government agents. This is so because the law of evidence inherently involves trade-offs between the needs of the judicial process and competing societal interests. But it is important to recognize that there is nothing unique about this feature of privileges.

A central question in assessing any such rule is how much relevant evidence will be lost if the rule is enacted. It is impossible to know this with any exactitude, because this inquiry invariably involves unprovable counterfactuals. But, as noted earlier, privileges have a distinctive feature in this regard that must be carefully considered.

If, in any given situation, we focus on the moment the privilege is invoked (for example, when the reporter refuses to disclose a source to a grand jury), the cost of the privilege will seem high, for we appear to be "losing" something quite tangible because of the privilege. But if we focus on the moment the source speaks with the reporter, we will see the matter quite differently.

Assume a particular source will not disclose confidential information to a reporter in the absence of a privilege. If there is no privilege, the source will not reveal the information, the reporter will not be able to publish the information, the reporter will not be called to testify before the grand jury, and the grand jury will not learn the source's identity. In this situation, the absence of the privilege will deprive the grand jury of the *exact same evidence* as the existence of the privilege. But at least with the privilege, the public and law enforcement will gain access to the underlying information through the newspaper report. In this situation, the privilege is *costless* to the legal system, and at the same time provides significant benefits both to law enforcement and the public.

Of course, some, perhaps many, sources will reveal information to a reporter even without a privilege. It is the evidentiary loss of *those* disclosures that is the true cost of the privilege. The same analysis holds for other privileges as well, such as attorney-client and doctor-patient. It is essential to examine the privilege in this manner in order to understand the actual impact of the journalist-source privilege.

Here are two ways to assess the relative costs and benefits. (1) On balance, it is probably the case that the most important confidential communications, the ones that are of greatest value to the public, are those that would get the source in the most "trouble." Thus, the absence of a privilege is most likely to chill the most valuable disclosures. (2) If one compares criminal prosecutions in states with an absolute privilege with those in states with only a qualified privilege, there is almost certainly no measurable difference in the effectiveness of law enforcement. Even though there may be a difference in the outcomes of a few idiosyncratic cases, the existence of even an absolute privilege probably has no discernable effect on the legal system *as a whole*. If we focus, as we should, on these large-scale effects, rather than on a few highly unusual cases when the issue captures the public's attention, it seems clear that the benefits we derive from the privilege significantly outweigh its negative effects on law enforcement. This is so because the percentage of cases in which the issue arises is vanishingly small[37] and because, in serious cases, prosecutors are almost always able to use alternative ways to investigate the crime.

My conclusion, then, like that of forty-nine states and the District of Columbia, is that public policy strongly supports a journalist-source privilege. Indeed, the absence of a federal journalist-source privilege seems inexplicable.

Framing a Federal Journalist-Source Privilege

Many issues arise in framing such a privilege. I will address three of them here: Who can invoke the privilege? Should the privilege be absolute? What if the disclosure by the source is itself a crime?

Who Can Invoke the Privilege?

At the outset, it must be recalled that the privilege belongs to the source, not to the reporter. When the reporter invokes the privilege, she is merely acting as the agent of the source.[38] With that in mind, the question should properly be rephrased as follows: To whom may a source properly disclose information in reasonable reliance that the disclosure will be protected by the journalist-source privilege?

As we saw in chapter 3, the answer should be a functional one. The focus should not be on whether the reporter fits within any particular category. Rather, a source should be protected whenever (a) he makes a confidential disclosure to an individual, (b) reasonably believing that the individual regularly disseminates information to the public, (c) when the source's purpose is to enable the individual to disseminate the information to the public.

Such a definition does not resolve every possible question. "Public," for example, should include specific communities, such as a university or a specialized set of readers. But the essence of the definition is clear. What we should be most concerned about are the *reasonable* expectations of the source, rather than the formal credentials of the recipient of the information.

Absolute or Qualified Privilege?

Thirty-six states have some form of qualified journalist-source privilege.[39] In these states, the government can require the journalist to reveal the confidential information if the government can show that it has exhausted alternative ways of obtaining the information and that the information is necessary to serve a substantial government interest.[40]

There are many variations of this formulation, but this is the essence of it. The logic of the qualified privilege is that it appears never to deny the government access to information that the government really "needs." Correlatively, it appears to protect the privilege when breaching it would serve no substantial government interest. As such, it appears to be a sensible compromise. Nothing could be farther from the truth.

Although the qualified privilege has a superficial appeal, it is misguided. It purports to achieve the best of both worlds, but probably achieves the opposite. For quite sensible reasons, other privileges, such as the attorney-client, doctor-patient, psychotherapist-patient, and priest-penitent privileges, which are deeply rooted in our national experience, do *not* allow such ad hoc determinations of "need" to override the privilege.[41]

The qualified privilege rests on the illusion that the costs and benefits of the privilege can properly be assessed at the moment the privilege is asserted.[42] But as I have indicated earlier, this is false. The real impact of the privilege must be assessed, not when the privilege is asserted, but when the source speaks with the reporter. By focusing on the wrong moment in time, the qualified privilege ignores the disclosures it *prevents* from ever occurring. That is, it disregards the cost to society of all the disclosures that sources *do not make* because they are chilled by the uncertainty of the qualified privilege. It is thus premised on a distorted "balancing" of the competing interests.

Moreover, the qualified privilege undermines the very purpose of the journalist-source privilege. Imagine yourself in the position of a source. You are a congressional staffer who has reason to believe a senator has taken a bribe. You want to reveal this to a journalist, but you do not want to be known as "loose-lipped" or "disloyal." You face the prospect of a qualified privilege. At the moment you speak with the reporter, it is impossible for you to know whether, several months hence, some prosecutor will or will not be able to make the requisite showing to pierce the privilege. This puts you in a craps-shoot.

But the very purpose of the privilege is to *encourage* sources to disclose useful information to the public. The uncertainty surrounding the qualified privilege undercuts this purpose and is unfair to sources, whose disclosures we are attempting to induce. In short, the qualified privilege is a bad business all around. And that is precisely why other privileges are not framed in this manner.

Does this mean the journalist-source privilege must be *absolute*? Thirteen states and the District of Columbia have reached this conclusion.[43] And, indeed, there is considerable virtue in a simple, straightforward, unambiguous privilege. But there may be *some* circumstances in which it seems sensible to breach the privilege.

For example, if a journalist broadcasts information, obtained from a confidential source, about a grave crime or serious breach of national security that is likely to occur imminently, it may seem irresponsible to protect the identity of the source. More concretely, suppose a reporter broadcasts a news alert that, according to a reliable, confidential source, a major terrorist attack will strike New York the next day, and law enforcement authorities want the reporter to reveal the name of the source so they can attempt to track him down and possibly prevent the attack. Is this a sufficiently compelling justification to override the privilege? It would certainly seem so, and this would be analogous to the rule in the psychotherapist-patient context that voids the privilege if the psychotherapist learns that her patient intends imminently to inflict serious harm on himself or others.[44]

But even in this situation the matter is not free from doubt. It must be borne in mind that, as a practical matter, without an absolute privilege the source might not be willing to disclose this information. Thus, in the long-run, this exception might hinder rather than help law enforcement. Public officials are better off knowing that a threat exists, even if they do not know the identity of the source, than knowing nothing at all. Thus, breaching the privilege in even this seemingly compelling situation might in the long-run prove counterproductive. It is for this reason that the attorney-client privilege generally provides that no showing of need is sufficient to pierce the privilege.[45] It may be too much to expect legislators not to create an exemption for imminent threats to the national security. Apart from this very narrowly defined exception, however, an absolute privilege will best serve the *overall* interests of society.

What If the Source's Disclosure Is Itself Unlawful?

An interesting twist occurs when the source's disclosure is itself a criminal act. Suppose, for example, a government employee unlawfully reveals to a reporter classified information that the United States has broken a terrorist code or confidential information about a private individual's tax return. As we have seen, the primary purpose of the privilege is to encourage sources to disclose information to journalists because such disclosures promote the public interest. But when the act of disclosure is itself unlawful, the law has already determined that the public interest cuts *against* disclosure. It would thus seem perverse to allow a journalist to shield the identity of a source whose disclosure is itself punishable as a criminal act. The goal of the privilege is to foster whistle-blowing and other lawful disclosures, not to encourage individuals to use the press to commit criminal acts.[46]

A rule that excluded all unlawful disclosures from the scope of the journalist-source privilege would be consistent with other privileges. A client who consults an attorney in order to figure out how to commit the perfect murder is not protected by the attorney-client privilege,[47] and a patient who consults a doctor in order to learn how best to defraud an insurance company is not protected by the doctor-patient privilege. This is so regardless of whether the attorney or doctor knew of the client's or patient's intent at the time of the conversation.[48] Such use of doctors and lawyers is not what those privileges are designed to encourage.

By the same reasoning, a source whose disclosure is unlawful is not engaging in conduct that society intends to encourage. To the contrary, the purpose of prohibiting the disclosure is to *discourage* such conduct. It would therefore seem sensible to conclude that a source whose disclosure is unlawful is not entitled to the protection of the journalist-source privilege.

There are, however, objections to such a limitation on the privilege. In some circumstances, it may not be clear to the reporter, or even to the source, whether the disclosure is unlawful. Because of the complexity of the relevant criminal statute, this may have been the case in the Lewis Libby/Judith Miller/Matt Cooper situation.[49] If the privilege does not cover unlawful disclosures, but it is unclear whether a particular disclosure is unlawful at the time it is made, how is the reporter to know whether to promise confidentiality?

The answer is simple. A promise of confidentiality should be understood as binding *only to the extent allowed by law*. Ultimately, it is for the court, not the reporter, to resolve this issue. The court should protect the privilege unless the source knew or should have known that the disclosure was unlawful.

A second objection to an unlawful disclosure limitation is that some unlawful disclosures are of substantial public value. The Pentagon Papers case[50] is a classic illustration. Although the government can ordinarily punish an employee who unlawfully leaks classified information,[51] it does not *necessarily* follow that the privilege should be breached if the information is of substantial value to the public. This is a difficult and tricky question.

In the context of unlawful leaks, the journalist-source privilege may be seen as an intermediate case. On the one hand, government employees ordinarily can be punished for violating reasonable confidentiality restrictions with respect to information they learn during the course of their employment.[52] On the other hand, the media ordinarily may publish information they learn from an unlawful leak, unless the publication creates a clear and present danger of a grave harm to the nation.[53] The journalist-source privilege falls between these two rules. Because the leak is unlawful, it seems perverse to shield the source's identity. But because the press has a constitutional right to publish the information, it seems perverse to require the press to identify the source.

The best resolution is to uphold the privilege if the unlawful leak discloses information of significant public value. This strikes a reasonable balance between full protection of the source's identity and no protection of his identity, based on the contribution of the leak to public debate. To illustrate what I mean by "significant public value," I would place the Pentagon Papers and the leak of the Abu Ghraib scandal[54] on one side of the line, and Lewis Libby's conversation with Matt Cooper about Valerie Plame[55] and James Taricani's leak of grand jury evidence in Rhode Island,[56] on the other.[57] Although this rule will inevitably involve some uncertainty in marginal cases, it would apply only when the leak is unlawful, so any chilling effect would be of relatively minor concern.

Notes

1. See, e.g., *Upjohn Co. v. United States*, 449 U.S. 383, 389 (1980).

2. See, e.g., *Trammel v. United States*, 445 U.S. 40, 51 (1980) (contrasting spousal privilege with other categories of testimonial privilege, including that applicable to physician-patient relationships).

3. See, e.g., *Jaffe v. Redmond*, 518 U.S. 1, 15 (1996).

4. See, e.g., *Trammel*, 445 U.S. at 53.

5. See *New York v. Phillips* (N.Y. Ct. Gen. Sess. 1813), reprinted in "Privileged Communications to Clergymen, 1 *Cath. Law.* 199-209 (1955).

6. See MODEL RULES OF PROF'L CONDUCT R. 1.6 (1983); see also N.Y. STATE BAR ASS'N, *Statement of Client's Rights* (2005) (adopting the standards suggested by the ABA).

7. See *Republic Gear Co. v. Borg-Warner Corp.*, 381 F.2d 551, 556 (2d Cir. 1967); 8 JOHN HENRY WIGMORE, EVIDENCE IN TRIALS AT COMMON LAW § 2321 (John T. McNaughton ed., 1961).

8. The attorney-client privilege is recognized in every jurisdiction in the United States. Other privileges are recognized in varying forms in different jurisdictions.

9. See, e.g., *Twentieth Century Music Corp. v. Aiken*, 422 U.S. 151, 156 (1975).

10. Thirty-one states have recognized the privilege by statute. See, ALA. CODE § 12-21-142 (2005); ALASKA STAT. § 09.25.320 (2005); ARIZ REV. STAT. § 12-2214 (LexisNexis, 2005); ARK. CODE ANN. § 16-85-510 (2005); CAL. EVID. CODE § 1070 (Deering, 2005); COLO. REV. STAT. § 13-90-119 (2005); DEL. CODE ANN. tit. 10 § 4321 (2005); FLA. STAT. ANN. § 90.5015 (LexisNexis, 2005); GA. CODE. ANN. § 24-9-30 (2005); 735 ILL. COMP. STAT. ANN. 5/8-901 (LexisNexis, 2005); IND. CODE ANN. § 34-46-4-2 (LexisNexis, 2005); KY. REV. STAT. ANN. § 421.100 (LexisNexis, 2005); LA. REV. STAT. ANN. § 45:1452 (2005); MD. CODE ANN., CTS. & JUD. PROC. § 9-112 (LexisNexis, 2005); MICH. COMP. LAWS SERV. § 767.5a (LexisNexis, 2005); MINN. STAT. § 595.022 (2004); MONT. CODE ANN. § 26-1-902 (2005); NEB. REV. STAT. ANN. § 20-144 (LexisNexis, 2005); NEV. REV. STAT. ANN. § 49.275 (LexisNexis, 2005); N.J. STAT. ANN. § 2A:84A-21.9 (West, 2005); N.M. STAT. ANN. § 38-6-7 (LexisNexis, 2005); N.Y. CIV. RIGHTS LAW § 79-h (2005); N.C. GEN. STAT. § 8-53.11 (2005); N.D. CENT. CODE § 31-01-06.2 (2005); OHIO REV. CODE ANN. § 2739.12 (LexisNexis, 2005); OKLA. STAT. ANN. tit. 12, § 2506 (West, 2004); OR. REV. STAT. § 44.520 (2003); 42 PA. CONS. STAT. § 5942 (2005); R.I. GEN. LAWS § 9-19.1-2 (2005); S.C. CODE ANN. § 19-11-100 (2004); TENN. CODE ANN. § 24-1-208 (2005). Eighteen states have recognized it by judicial decision. See, e.g., Jean-Paul Jassy, "The Prosecutor's Subpoena and the Reporter's Privilege," *Commc'n. Law.*, Winter 2000, at n.25, *available at* www.abanet.org/forums/communication/comlawyer/winter00/jassy.html (citing to case law of eight states that have recognized the privilege via judicial decision). The only state that has not recognized the privilege in any form is Wyoming.

11. See *Branzburg v. Hayes*, 408 U.S. 665, 697 (1972).

12. See, e.g., *United States v. Hammad*, 846 F.2d 854, 859 (2d Cir. 1988) (citing *McNabb v. United States*, 318 U.S. 332, 340 (1943)).

13. Civil Rights Act of 1964, Pub. L. No. 88-352, 78 Stat. 241 (codified as amended in scattered sections of the U.S.C.).

14. See, e.g., 18 U.S.C. § 2511(1) (2000).

15. See, e.g., 26 U.S.C. § 501(c)(3) (2000).

16. See, e.g., 22 U.S.C. § 4086 (2000).

17. See, e.g., Fred C. Zacharias, "Rethinking Confidentiality," 74 *Iowa L. Rev.* 351, 356 (1988) (noting that the attorney-client privilege "protects clients and benefits society by enabling the legal system to work").

18. 408 U.S. 665 (1972).

19. See id. at 667.

20. Id. at 743 (Stewart, J., dissenting) (citation omitted).

21. Id. at 707-708.

22. See id. at 709 (Powell, J., concurring).

23. Id. at 710.

24. Building upon Justice Powell's concurring opinion in *Branzburg*, most federal courts of appeals have held that the First Amendment protects some form of journalist-source privilege. See, e.g., *LaRouche v. Nat'l Broad. Co.*, 780 F.2d 1134, 1139 (4th Cir. 1986); *United States v. Caporale*, 806 F.2d 1487, 1504 (11th Cir. 1986); *Zerilli v. Smith*, 656 F.2d 705, 711-12 (D.C. Cir. 1981); *Bruno & Stillman, Inc. v. Globe Newspaper Co.*, 633 F.2d 583, 594-95 (1st

Cir. 1980); *United States v. Criden*, 633 F.2d 346, 357 (3d Cir. 1980); *Miller v. Transamerican Press, Inc.*, 621 F.2d 721, 725 (5th Cir. 1980); *Silkwood v. Kerr-McGee Corp.*, 563 F.2d 433, 437 (10th Cir. 1977); *Farr v. Pitchess*, 522 F.2d 464, 467 (9th Cir. 1975); *Baker v. F & F Investment*, 470 F.2d 778, 784 (2d Cir. 1972).

25. Compare OHIO REV. CODE ANN. § 2739.04 (LexisNexis 2005) (protecting the source of the information), with OKLA. STAT. ANN. tit. 12, § 2506 (2004) (protecting unpublished information, as well as the source).

26. *See Branzburg*, 408 U.S. at 684 (providing "that the First Amendment does not guarantee the press a constitutional right of special access to information not available to the public generally"); see also id. at 682 (noting "that the First Amendment does not invalidate every incidental burdening of the press that may result from the enforcement of civil or criminal statutes of general applicability").

27. See id. at 682.

28. See generally *Cohen v. California*, 403 U.S. 15 (1971); *Terminiello v. City of Chicago*, 337 U.S. 1, 2-3 (1949).

29. See generally *Texas v. Johnson*, 491 U.S. 397, 402-06 (1989); *United States v. O'Brien*, 391 U.S. 367, 385 (1968).

30. See, e.g., *NAACP v. Alabama*, 357 U.S. 449, 462-63 (1958) (holding that for the state to require the NAACP to disclose its membership lists in Alabama at the height of the civil rights movement would effectively destroy the NAACP's ability to operate).

31. See, e.g., *Arcara v. Cloud Books, Inc.*, 478 U.S. 697, 707 (1986) (upholding as an "incidental" restriction on speech a law requiring the closing of any building used for prostitution, as applied to an "adult" bookstore); *Wayte v. United States*, 470 U.S. 598, 614 (1985) (upholding as an "incidental" restriction on speech the government's policy of enforcing the selective service registration requirement only against those men who advised the government that they had failed to register or who were reported by others as having failed to register); *Citizen Publishing Co. v. United States*, 394 U.S. 131, 139 (1969) (upholding the Sherman Antitrust Act, as applied to the press); *O'Brien*, 391 U.S. at 385 (upholding as an "incidental" restriction on speech a federal law prohibiting any individual to destroy a draft card, as applied to an individual who burned a draft card to protest the Vietnam War); *Oklahoma Press Publishing Co. v. Walling*, 327 U.S. 186, 193 (1946) (upholding the Fair Labor Standards Act, as applied to the press); see generally Geoffrey R. Stone, "Content-Neutral Restrictions," 54 *U. Chi. L. Rev.* 46, 99-114 (1987).

32. See, e.g., *Cohen v. Cowles Media Co.*, 501 U.S. 663, 669-70 (1991); *Associated Press v. NLRB*, 301 U.S. 103, 132-33 (1937).

33. *Branzburg v. Hayes*, 408 U.S. 665, 682 (1972).

34. Id. at 704.

35. See, e.g., 47 U.S.C. § 151 (2000).

36. See, e.g., *Turner Broad. Sys., Inc. v. FCC*, 512 U.S. 622, 643-45 (1994) (upholding "must carry" provisions that favored broadcast over cable programmers); *Leathers v. Medlock*, 499 U.S. 439, 444 (1991) (upholding a state law exempting newspapers and magazines but not cable television from a gross receipts tax); *Red Lion Broad. Co. v. FCC*, 395 U.S. 367, 386-87 (1969) (upholding regulations for broadcasting that would be unconstitutional for print media).

37. For example, a LexisNexis search for cases in New York state—a state with a statutory shield law—using the terms "confidential and OVERVIEW (§ 79-h)" during the time period spanning January 1975 and January 1990, produces sixteen results. LEXISNEXIS:

NY STATE CASES, COMBINED Database (last searched Nov. 1, 2005), *available at* LEX-ISNEXIS:NYCTS/search: "confidential and overview (sec 79-h) and date (geq (1/1/1975) and leq (1/1/1990))." However, a search for cases during the subsequent fifteen-year period, January 1990 through January 2005, produces only seven results. LEXISNEXIS: NY STATE CASES, COMBINED Database (last searched Nov. 1, 2005), *available at* LEXISNEXIS: NYCTS/search: "confidential and overview (sec 79-h) and date (geq (1/1/1990) and leq (1/1/2005))".

38. In several cases, courts have held that the journalist-source privilege belongs to the reporter and cannot be waived by the source. See, e.g., *United States v. Cuthbertson*, 630 F.2d 139, 147 (3d Cir. 1980); *Palandjian v. Pahlavi*, 103 F.R.D. 410, 413 (D.D.C. 1984); *Los Angeles Mem'l Coliseum Comm'n v. NFL*, 89 F.R.D. 489, 494 (C.D. Cal. 1981). This view of the privilege seems to assume that the primary purpose of the privilege is to maintain the independence of the press rather than to encourage open communication by sources. This view makes sense insofar as the issue is whether journalists should enjoy a "work product" privilege analogous to the attorney's work product doctrine. To the extent such a doctrine applies to journalists, it would then be necessary to define precisely who is a journalist. Proposals for a "work product" doctrine for journalists generally assume that a qualified privilege would be adequate to protect this interest, as it is in the attorney work product situation. See, e.g., Free Speech Protection Act of 2005, S. 369, 109th Cong. (2005) (proposed by Senator Christopher Dodd).

On the attorney work product doctrine, see *Hickman v. Taylor*, 329 U.S. 495, 510-11 (1947).

"[I]t is essential that a lawyer work with a certain degree of privacy, free from unnecessary intrusion by opposing parties and their counsel. Proper preparation of a client's case demands that he assemble information, sift what he considers to be the relevant from the irrelevant facts, prepare his legal theories and plan his strategy without undue and needless interference. . . . This work is reflected, of course, in interviews, statements, memoranda, correspondence, briefs, mental impressions, personal beliefs, and countless other tangible and intangible ways. . . . Were such materials open to opposing counsel on mere demand, much of what is now put down in writing would remain unwritten. An attorney's thoughts, heretofore inviolate, would not be his own. Inefficiency, unfairness, and sharp practices would inevitably develop in the giving of legal advice and in the preparation of cases for trial. The effect on the legal profession would be demoralizing. And the interests of the clients and the cause of justice would be poorly served." Id.

39. Eighteen states have a qualified statutory privilege, including Alaska, Arizona, Arkansas, Colorado, Florida, Georgia, Illinois, Louisiana, Michigan, Minnesota, New Jersey, New Mexico, North Carolina, North Dakota, Oklahoma, Rhode Island, South Carolina, and Tennessee. Another eighteen states have a qualified judicial privilege. See supra note 10.

40. See, e.g., COLO. REV. STAT. § 13-90-119 (2005); FLA. STAT. ANN. § 90.5015 (LexisNexis, 2005).

41. See, e.g., *Jaffee v. Redmond*, 518 U.S. 1, 2, 17-18 (1995).

42. See id. at 2, 17-18; Anne W. Robinson, "Evidentiary Privileges and the Exclusionary Rule: Dual Justifications for an Absolute Rape Victim Counselor Privilege," 31 *New Eng. J. Crim. & Civ. Confinement*, 331, 338 (2005).

43. The thirteen states with an absolute privilege are Alaska, Delaware, Indiana, Kentucky, Maryland, Montana, Nebraska, Nevada, New York, Ohio, Oregon, and Pennsylvania.

44. See e.g., *United States v. Chase*, 340 F.3d 978, 984 (9th Cir. 2003) (noting that "[m]ost states have a dangerous-patient exception to their psychotherapist-patient confidentiality laws").

45. See, e.g., *Admiral Ins. Co. v. U.S. Dist. Court*, 881 F.2d 1486, 1495 (9th Cir. 1989) (opining that the attorney-client privilege cannot be vitiated by a claim that the information sought is unavailable from any other source, for "[s]uch an exception either would destroy the privilege or render it so tenuous and uncertain that it would be 'little better than no privilege at all'").

46. An interesting question is whether the same principle should apply when the leak is not a crime, but a tort. For example, suppose a confidential source makes a false statement of fact to a newspaper, which publishes the statement, attributing it to a confidential source. Can the newspaper be compelled to reveal the identity of the source on the theory that there is no public policy to encourage people to make false statements of fact to newspapers?

47. See, e.g., *Clark v. United States*, 289 U.S. 1, 15 (1933); Harry I. Subin, "The Lawyer as Superego: Disclosure of Client Confidences to Prevent Harm," 70 *Iowa L. Rev.* 1091, 1113-17 (1985).

48. See, e.g., *Nix v. Whiteside*, 475 U.S. 157, 167 (1986) (noting that professional standards for attorneys prohibit assisting conduct they *know* to be illegal).

49. See Jim VandeHei and Mike Allen, "Bush Raises Threshold for Firing Aides in Leak Probe," *Washington Post*, July 19, 2005, at A01; see also Michael Duffy, "Let's Make a Deal," *Time*, Oct. 10, 2005, at 15; Diedtra Henderson, "Reporter Ties Cheney Aide to CIA Story," *Boston Globe*, July 18, 2005, at A1; Anne E. Kornblut, "At Milestone in Inquiry, Rove, and the G.O.P., Breathe a Bit Easier," *New York Times*, Oct. 29, 2005, at A1.

50. *New York Times Co. v. United States*, 403 U.S. 713 (1971) (per curiam).

51. It is important to note that if the leaker cannot constitutionally be punished for the leak, then the leak is not unlawful, and this entire analysis is irrelevant.

52. See, e.g., *Snepp v. United States*, 444 U.S. 507, 507-08, 510 (1980) (per curiam) (upholding a restriction on the publication by a former CIA agent of information learned during the course of his employment by the CIA).

53. See, e.g., *Landmark Commc'ns, Inc. v. Virginia*, 435 U.S. 829, 845 (1978) (holding that the government cannot prohibit the publication of confidential information); *Nebraska Press Ass'n v. Stuart*, 427 U.S. 539, 570 (1976) (holding that the government cannot prohibit the publication of confessions and other facts strongly implicative of the accused in a criminal case); *New York Times Co.*, 403 U.S. at 714 (holding that the government could not enjoin publication of the Pentagon Papers).

54. See, e.g., Dana Priest and Joe Stephens, "Secret World of U.S. Interrogation," *Washington Post*, May 11, 2004, at A1.

55. See *In re Grand Jury Subpoena, Judith Miller*, 397 F.3d 964, 966-67 (D.C. Cir. 2005); David Johnston and Richard W. Stevenson, "Prosecutor Narrows Focus on Rove Role in C.I.A. Leak," *New York Times*, Nov. 4, 2005, at A1.

56. See *In re Special Proceedings*, 373 F.3d 37, 40-41 (1st Cir. 2004).

57. This is a higher standard of newsworthiness than the Supreme Court has applied in deciding when the press has a First Amendment right to publish or broadcast information obtained from unlawful sources. See *Bartnicki v. Vopper*, 532 U.S. 514, 534-35 (2001) (holding that a radio commentator could not constitutionally be held liable for damages for broadcasting an unlawfully recorded telephone call, where the broadcast involved "truthful information of public concern").

Conclusion

A S this book suggests, it is not easy to reconcile the nation's important interest in security with its equally important interest in preserving a free and responsible press and an informed citizenry. In summary, my conclusions are as follows:

- The government can constitutionally criminally punish a public employee who knowingly discloses classified information to a journalist for the purpose of publication if the information was not previously in the public domain and its disclosure has the potential to harm the national security, unless the disclosure reveals unlawful government action and the employee has complied with reasonable whistle-blower procedures governing the disclosure of such information.
- The government can constitutionally punish the press for publishing classified information if the publisher knew that (a) it was publishing classified information, (b) the publication of which would likely result in imminent and grave harm to the national security, and (c) the publication would not meaningfully contribute to public debate.
- The government can constitutionally punish a journalist for bribing, coercing, or defrauding a public employee into disclosing classified information if the employee could constitutionally be punished for disclosing the information.

- The government can constitutionally punish a journalist for receiving or soliciting the disclosure of classified information from a public employee if the journalist (a) expressly incited the employee unlawfully to disclose classified information; (b) knowing that publication of the information would result in likely, imminent, and grave harm to the national security; and (c) knowing that publication of the information would not meaningfully contribute to public debate.
- The government should have the authority to compel a journalist to reveal the identity of a confidential source only if (a) it can convincingly demonstrate that it needs the information to prevent an imminent and grave crime or threat to the national security, or (b) the disclosure was clearly unlawful and did not significantly contribute to public debate.

It is surely tempting simply to err on the side of government secrecy. But as the Declaration of Independence stated, a free society must rest on "the consent of the governed." There is no meaningful consent when "those who are governed do not know to what they are consenting."[1]

Note

1. David Wise and Thomas B. Ross, *The Invisible Government*, 6 (New York: Random House, 1964).

The Statutory Framework

By Stephen I. Vladeck, University of Miami School of Law

THE United States has never had its own version of the United Kingdom's "Official Secrets Act"—the name given to a comprehensive series of acts of Parliament dating back to 1911 that, in broad terms, prohibit the retention and/or dissemination of numerous forms of sensitive governmental information, including by the press.[1] Instead, the U.S. Congress has traditionally focused its attention on more discrete targets, punishing the dissemination of very specific types of sensitive governmental information (in many cases, by specific classes of individuals). As such, the statutory framework governing the complicated balance between governmental secrecy and the freedom of the press in the United States is little more than a disorganized amalgamation of unconnected statutes. Some of the provisions overlap each other and border on redundancy. Others are difficult to parse, and cannot possibly prohibit what their plain language appears to suggest. Still others, when read together, seem to promote mutually inconsistent policy goals.

And yet, whereas the statutory framework is not necessarily coherent, recent cases, in particular the case involving American Israel Public Affairs Committee (AIPAC) in the U.S. District Court for the Eastern District of Virginia,[2] testify to the importance of understanding its different components in their entireties. The lack of clarity notwithstanding, there are numerous statutes under which the press may find itself liable for the gathering and reporting of stories implicating governmental secrecy, especially as courts increasingly embrace theories of third-party inchoate liability, as in the AIPAC case.

The Espionage Act

From the Sedition Act of 1798,[3] which expired in 1801, through the outbreak of World War I, there was virtually no federal legislation prohibiting seditious expression, including the dissemination and/or publication of information harmful to the national defense.[4] Contemporaneously with the United States' entry into the war, however, Congress enacted the Espionage Act of 1917,[5] which, except for the amendments discussed below, remains on the books largely in its original form today at 18 U.S.C. §§ 793 et seq. Written primarily by then-Assistant Attorney General Charles Warren, the Act included a number of seemingly overlapping and often ambiguous provisions.

The Knowledge Requirement

Section 793(a), which derives from section 1(a) of the Espionage Act, prohibits obtaining information concerning a series of national defense installations—places—"with intent or reason to believe that the information is to be used to the injury of the United States, or to the advantage of any foreign nation." Similarly, § 793(b) prohibits individuals with similar intent "or reason to believe" from copying, taking, making, or obtaining "any sketch, photograph, photographic negative, blueprint, plan, map, model, instrument, appliance, document, writing, or note of *anything* connected with the national defense" (emphasis added). Although an early legal challenge argued the requirement that the information at issue be "connected with the national defense" was unconstitutionally vague, the Supreme Court read a scienter requirement into the statute (and thus upheld it) in *Gorin v. United States* in 1941.[6]

Because of the Supreme Court's decision in *Gorin* (which also held that the Act likely could not prohibit the collection of public information[7]), §§ 793(a) and 793(b) are unlikely candidates for potential press liability under the Espionage Act. The mere gathering and/or publication of the information specified in the two provisions would only sustain charges under the Act if the reporter at issue had "intent or reason to believe that the information to be obtained is to be used to the injury of the United States, or to the advantage of any foreign nation." Thus, the scienter requirement read into these provisions in *Gorin* renders potential press liability under §§ 793(a) and 793(b) somewhat unlikely.

Application to Those with Unauthorized Access to Information

Section 793(c) is, in important ways, far broader. The ancestor of section 1(c) of the Espionage Act, the provision creates criminal liability for any individual who "receives or obtains or agrees or attempts to receive or obtain from any person, or from any source whatever" various material related to the national defense, so long as the individual "know[s] or ha[s] reason to believe, at the time he receives or obtains [the information] . . . that it has been or will be obtained, taken, made, or disposed of by any person contrary to the provisions of [the Espionage Act]." Thus, whereas §§ 793(a) and 793(b) prohibit the collection of secret information relating to the national defense, § 793(c) prohibits the receipt of such information, or even attempts at receipt thereof, so long as the recipient does or should have knowledge that the source, in obtaining the information, violated some other provision of the Espionage Act.

In addition, whereas §§ 793(d) and 793(f) prohibit the dissemination of national security information that is in the lawful possession of the individual who disseminates it (§ 793(d) prohibits willful communication; § 793(f) prohibits negligence), § 793(e)—which, like §§ 793(d) and 793(f), derives from § 1(d) of the Espionage Act[8]—prohibits the same by an individual who has unauthorized possession of the information at issue.

Thus, in sweeping language, § 793(e) prohibits individuals from willfully communicating—or attempting to communicate—to any person not entitled to receive it "any document, writing, code book, signal book, sketch, photograph, photographic negative, blueprint, plan, map, model, instrument, appliance, or note relating to the national defense, or information relating to the national defense which information the possessor has reason to believe could be used to the injury of the United States or to the advantage of any foreign nation." Section 793(e) goes one important step further, however, for it also prohibits the retention of such information and the concomitant failure to deliver such information "to the officer or employee of the United States entitled to receive it."

Section 793(e) therefore appears to have a far more relaxed intent requirement than §§ 793(a) and 793(b). The provision does not require specific intent so long as the communication or retention of classified information is willful. From the perspective of the press, then, § 793(e) is easily one of the most significant provisions in the debate over governmental secrecy versus freedom of the press, and has received the most attention in judicial and scholarly discussions of the Act and its potential constitutional infirmities, most famously in the various opinions in the Pentagon Papers case.[9] Perhaps most succinctly, it was recently described as "pretty much one of the scariest statutes around,"[10] at least largely because of the lack of a specific intent requirement.

Concerns over the scope of § 793(e) may be bolstered by the Eastern District of Virginia's recent decision in the AIPAC case,[11] sustaining, for perhaps the first time, the liability of third parties (albeit, not the press) for conspiring to violate §§ 793(d) and 793(e), and, in the defendant's case, for aiding and abetting a violation of § 793(d). As Judge Ellis concluded, "The conclusion here is that the balance struck by § 793 between these competing interests is constitutionally permissible because (1) it limits the breadth of the term 'related to the national defense' to matters closely held by the government for the legitimate reason that their disclosure could threaten our collective security; and (2) it imposes rigorous scienter requirements as a condition for finding criminal liability."[12]

Provisions That Prohibit Publication

A number of judges and scholars have argued against the applicability of § 793(e) to the press in the absence of an express reference to the "publication" of such secret national security information. By comparison, three separate provisions of the Espionage Act do expressly prohibit the publication of particular national defense information.

First, § 794(b) applies to "Whoever, in time of war, with intent that the same shall be communicated to the enemy, collects, records, publishes, or communicates . . . [the disposition of armed forces] or any other information relating to the public defense, which might be useful to the enemy." Although the provision might appear to turn on whether it is a "time of war," § 798(a) expands § 794(b) to apply so long as various national emergencies remain in place, a provision that remains satisfied today. On the merits, though, could the requisite intent be inferred from the act of publication itself?

Second, § 797 applies to whoever "reproduces, publishes, sells, or gives away" photographs of specified defense installations, unless the photographs were properly censored. Third, § 798(a), which generally relates to cryptography and was passed in 1950 at least largely in response to the *Chicago Tribune* incident from World War II, applies to whoever "communicates, furnishes, transmits, or otherwise makes available . . . or publishes" various prohibited materials, including "classified information . . . concerning the communication intelligence activities of the United States or any foreign government."[13] Section 798(b) defines "classified information" as "information which, at the time of a violation of this section, is, for reasons of national security, specifically designated by a United States Government Agency for limited or restricted dissemination or distribution."

In addition to the three codified provisions of the Espionage Act that expressly prohibit the act of publication, those who argue against the applicability of other provisions of the Act to the press often invoke language in one of the early drafts of the Espionage Act that was rejected by Congress. It would have provided that:

> During any national emergency resulting from a war to which the United States is a party, or from threat of such a war, the President may, by proclamation, declare the existence of such emergency and, by proclamation, prohibit the publishing or communicating of, or the attempting to publish or communicate any information relating to the national defense which, in his judgment, is of such character that it is or might be useful to the enemy.[14]

As Justice Douglas noted in his concurrence in the Pentagon Papers case, the provision was rejected by the Senate at least largely on First

Amendment grounds, and therefore militates against a construction of those enacted provisions that do not expressly reference "publishing" as applying to the press.[15]

Publication as Communication to a Foreign Government

One other noteworthy provision of the Espionage Act is 18 U.S.C. § 794(a), which applies to "Whoever, with intent or reason to believe that it is to be used to the injury of the United States or to the advantage of a foreign nation, communicates, delivers, or transmits . . . to any foreign government, or to any faction or party or military or naval force within a foreign country, . . . any document, . . . [other physical items], or information relating to the national defense." Thus, there is at least a plausible argument that the publication of certain national security information would constitute the communication of such information to a foreign government, and the issue, once again, would turn solely on whether the publisher had "intent or reason to believe that it is to be used to the injury of the United States or to the advantage of a foreign nation." Owing to the similarities in statutory language, would the scienter requirement from *Gorin* apply to a prosecution under this section?

Overlapping § 794(a) is 50 U.S.C. § 783, enacted as part of the 1950 amendments to the Espionage Act,[16] which provides that:

> It shall be unlawful for any officer or employee of the United States or of any department or agency thereof . . . to communicate in any manner or by any means, to any other person whom such officer or employee knows or has reason to believe to be an agent or representative of any foreign government, any information of a kind which shall have been classified by the President . . . as affecting the security of the United States, knowing or having reason to know that such information has been so classified, unless such officer or employee shall have been specifically authorized by the President, or by the head of the department, agency, or corporation by which this officer or employee is employed, to make such disclosure of such information.

Inchoate Liability and the Press

Finally, it bears noting that the Espionage Act also contains two independent conspiracy provisions. Pursuant to § 793(g), "If two or more persons conspire to violate any of the foregoing provisions of this section, and one or more of such persons do any act to effect the object of the conspiracy, each of the parties to such conspiracy shall be subject to the punishment provided for the offense which is the object of such conspiracy." Section 794(c) is to similar effect.

It is in the context of the conspiracy provisions that the potential liability of the press for the publication of governmental secrets becomes a much more troubling issue. Leaving aside the individual liability of the press for the act of publication, § 793(e) prohibits the unauthorized receipt of certain national security secrets, and other provisions of the Act prohibit, in broader strokes, the obtaining of such information. Thus, one of the central issues that may surface in a future prosecution of the press under the Espionage Act is inchoate liability—whether the reporters are liable either as coconspirators, or for aiding and abetting the individuals who provided the protected information.[17] Because such liability would attach to the possession of information, and not to its publication per se, the potential protections of the First Amendment's Press Clause are, at the very minimum, not as clearly established,[18] and may not provide much protection at all.[19]

Other Important Statutes

The Espionage Act, while constituting an important subset of statutes at issue in the balance between governmental secrecy and the freedom of the press, is a subset nonetheless. When considered in conjunction with the inchoate liability issue noted above, the other statutes should provide just as much cause for concern as the more open-ended provisions of the Espionage Act.

Stealing for the Press Is No Defense

First, and perhaps most importantly, is 18 U.S.C. § 641, one of the statutes at issue (along with §§ 793(d) and 793(e)) in the famous case of *United States v. Morison*.[20] Originally enacted in 1875,[21] § 641 applies to

Whoever . . . knowingly converts to his use or the use of another, or without authority, sells, conveys or disposes of any record, voucher, money, or thing of value of the United States or of any department or agency thereof . . . ;

or

Whoever receives, conceals, or retains the same with intent to convert it to his use or gain, knowing it to have been embezzled, stolen, purloined or converted . . .

Thus, § 641, in general terms, prohibits the conversion of any "thing of value" to the U.S. government, and also prohibits the knowing receipt of the same, "with intent to convert it to his use or gain."

Relying on § 641, the government prosecuted Samuel Morison for transmitting photographs of a new Soviet aircraft carrier to *Jane's Defence Weekly*, an English publisher of defense information. As the court noted, "The defendant would deny the application of [§ 641] to his theft because he says that he did not steal the material 'for private, covert use in illegal enterprises' but in order to give it to the press for public dissemination and information. . . . The mere fact that one has stolen a document in order that he may deliver it to the press, whether for money or for other personal gain, will not immunize him from responsibility for his criminal act."[22] In one exceptional case, a district court even held that using a government photocopier to make copies of government-owned documents could trigger liability under § 641.[23]

Considered in conjunction with the discussion of inchoate liability above, the potential liability under § 641 for reporters may be just as broad, if not broader, than the liability under §§ 793(d) and 793(e). As Judge Winter worried in *United States v. Truong*:

[B]ecause the statute was not drawn with the unauthorized disclosure of government information in mind, § 641 is not carefully crafted to specify exactly when disclosure of government information is illegal. The crucial language is "without authority." The precise contours of that phrase are not self-evident. This ambiguity is particularly disturbing because government information forms the basis of much of the discussion of public issues and, as a result, the unclear language of the statute threatens to impinge upon rights protected by the first amendment. Under § 641 as it is written, ... upper level government employees might use their discretion in an arbitrary fashion to prevent the disclosure of government information; and government employees, newspapers, and others could not be confident in many circumstances that the disclosure of a particular piece of government information was "authorized" within the meaning of § 641. Thus, the vagueness of the "without authority" standard could pose a serious threat to public debate of national issues, thereby bringing the constitutional validity of § 641 into question because of its chilling effect on the exercise of first amendment rights.[24]

Publication of Information by Government Employees

Also relevant to any discussion of freedom of the press and governmental secrecy are 18 U.S.C. §§ 952 and 1924. Enacted in 1933,[25] § 952 relates specifically to diplomatic codes and correspondence, and applies to "Whoever, by virtue of his employment by the United States, obtains from another or has or has had custody of or access to, any official diplomatic code or any matter prepared in any such code, ... without authorization or competent authority, [and] willfully publishes or furnishes to another any such code or matter, or any matter which was obtained while in the process of transmission between any foreign government and its diplomatic mission in the United States." A fair reading of the statute is that it prohibits the publication by the government employee, and not by an independent third party, but inchoate liability could still lead to liability for press reporting on encrypted communications between the United States and foreign governments or its overseas missions.

In the same vein is 18 U.S.C. § 1924, enacted in 1994,[26] which prohibits the unauthorized removal and retention of classified documents or material. It applies to "Whoever, being an officer, employee, contractor, or consultant of the United States, and, by virtue of his office, employment, position, or contract, becomes possessed of documents or materials containing classified information of the United States, [who] knowingly removes such documents or materials without authority and with the intent to retain such documents or materials at an unauthorized location."

Additional Relevant Statutes

Not to be overlooked are three other statutes dealing with more specific types of secret information. First among these is the Atomic Energy Act of 1954, 42 U.S.C. §§ 2011 et seq. Sections 2274, 2275, and 2277 thereof prohibit the communication, receipt, and disclosure, respectively, of "Restricted Data," which is defined as "all data concerning (1) design, manufacture, or utilization of atomic weapons; (2) the production of special nuclear material; or (3) the use of special nuclear material in the production of energy, but shall not include data declassified or removed from the Restricted Data category pursuant to section 2162 of this title."[27] In the *Progressive* case, in which the U.S. government successfully enjoined the publication of an article titled "The H-Bomb Secret: How We Got It, Why We're Telling It," it was a potential violation of § 2274(b) that formed the basis for the injunction.[28]

A very different statute, and one arguably of more relevance for contemporary purposes, is the Intelligence Identities Protection Act of 1982, 50 U.S.C. §§ 421 et seq. Section 421, specifically, prohibits the disclosure of information relating to the identity of covert agents. Whereas §§ 421(a) and 421(b) prohibit the disclosure of such information by individuals authorized to have access to classified information identifying the agent, § 421(c) applies to anyone who "discloses any information that identifies an individual as a covert agent to any individual not authorized to receive classified information, knowing that the information disclosed so identifies such individual and that the United States is taking affirmative measures to conceal such individual's classified intelligence relationship to the United States." The individual must intend "to identify and expose covert agents and [have] reason to believe that such activities would impair or impede the foreign intelligence activities of the United States." Importantly, though, § 421(c) "does not predicate liability on either access to or publication of classified information."[29]

Finally, the Invention Secrecy Act of 1951, 35 U.S.C. §§ 181 et seq., protects the disclosure of information relating to patents under "secrecy" orders. The statutory punishment, however, for disclosure of information relating to a patent under a secrecy order is forfeiture of the patent.[30] No criminal liability appears to attach to such disclosures.

Conclusion

In sum, then, the statutory framework appertaining to the balance between governmental secrecy and freedom of the press presents far more questions than answers. Owing to the dearth of significant case law interpreting the more ambiguous—and potentially controversial—provisions of the Espionage Act, and owing to the absence of a coherent, overarching statute governing the publication of national security information generally, the statutory framework provides an unsatisfactory lens through which to understand the background legal issues.

Insofar as principal liability is concerned, the central statutes to focus on are 18 U.S.C. §§ 641 and 793(e), particularly in light of the interpretation of § 793(e) adopted in the AIPAC case in August 2006. But as suggested above, the inchoate liability issues are perhaps more substantial going forward, especially to the extent that inchoate liability would arguably provide a means around the constitutional protections of the Press Clause.

Lastly, a separate point not considered here is the scope of (and availability of legal challenges to) the meaning of "classified" information within the various provisions discussed above. Especially where the statutes reference the dissemination of information to "those not entitled to receive it," who, precisely, does that term describe? These issues are heretofore unresolved in the case law, but could potentially pose additional problems in press-related prosecutions.

Notes

1. Official Secrets Act, 1911, 1 & 2 Geo. 5, c. 28 (Eng.); see also Official Secrets Act, 1989, c. 6 (Eng.); Official Secrets Act, 1920, 10 & 11 Geo. 5, c. 75 (Eng.).

2. See *United States v. Rosen*, No. 1:05-cr-225, 2006 WL 2345914 (E.D. Va. Aug. 9, 2006).

3. Act of July 14, 1798, ch. 74, 1 Stat. 596 (expired 1801).

4. For one of the few counterexamples, see Act of Mar. 3, 1911, ch. 226, 36 Stat. 1084 (prohibiting the disclosure of certain national defense secrets) (repealed 1917).

5. Act of June 15, 1917, ch. 30, 40 Stat. 217.

6. 312 U.S. 19, 27-28 (1941) ("The obvious delimiting words in the statute are those requiring 'intent or reason to believe that the information to be obtained is to be used to the injury of the United States, or to the advantage of any foreign nation'"); see also *United*

States v. Truong, 629 F.2d 908, 918 (4th Cir. 1980) (discussing *Gorin*'s scienter requirement); *In re Squillacote*, 790 A.2d 514, 519 (D.C. 2002) (per curiam) (same).

7. See 312 U.S. at 27-28; see also *United States v. Heine*, 151 F.2d 813 (2d Cir. 1945) (L. Hand, J.).

8. The three provisions were modified and separated by the Subversive Activities Control Act of 1950, Pub. L. No. 81-831, tit. I, § 18, 64 Stat. 987, 1004.

9. *New York Times Co. v. United States*, 403 U.S. 713 (1971) (per curiam).

10. Susan Buckley, *Reporting on the War on Terror: The Espionage Act and Other Scary Statutes* (New York: Media Law Resource Center, 2006), 7.

11. *United States v. Rosen*, No. 1:05-cr-225, 2006 WL 2345914 (E.D. Va. Aug. 9, 2006).

12. Id. at *31.

13. See, e.g., *New York Times*, 403 U.S. at 720-21 (Douglas, J., concurring). But see id. at 737-40 and nn.8-10 (White, J., concurring) (arguing that the *New York Times* and the *Washington Post* could constitutionally have been prosecuted for violating § 793(e)).

14. See 55 Cong. Rec. 1763 (1917).

15. See *New York Times*, 403 U.S. at 721-22 (citing 55 Cong. Rec. 2167 (1917)).

16. See supra note 8.

17. See generally 18 U.S.C. § 2 (aiding and abetting); id. § 371 (conspiracy).

18. See *First Nat'l Bank of Boston v. Bellotti*, 435 U.S. 765, 799-800 (1978) (Burger, C. J., concurring) ("The Speech Clause standing alone may be viewed as a protection of the liberty to express ideas and beliefs, while the Press Clause focuses specifically on the liberty to disseminate expression broadly and 'comprehends every sort of publication which affords a vehicle of information and opinion.'" (citation and footnote omitted)).

19. The Press Clause arguably is implicated only when the enforcement of governmental secrecy impacts the press itself. See Louis Henkin, "The Right to Know and the Duty to Withhold: The Case of the Pentagon Papers," 120 *U. Pa. L. Rev.* 271, 277 (1971).

20. 844 F.2d 1057 (4th Cir. 1988).

21. See Act of Mar. 3, 1875, ch. 144, 18 Stat. 479.

22. *Morison*, 844 F.2d at 1077.

23. See *United States v. Hubbard*, 474 F. Supp. 64 (D.D.C. 1979).

24. *United States v. Truong*, 629 F.2d 908, 924-25 (4th Cir. 1980) (citations and footnote omitted).

25. See Act of June 10, 1933, c. 57, 48 Stat. 122, 122-23.

26. Intelligence Authorization Act for FY1995, Pub. L. No. 103-359, § 808(a), 108 Stat. 3423, 3453 (1994).

27. 42 U.S.C. § 2014(y).

28. See *United States v. The Progressive, Inc.*, 467 F. Supp. 990, 993-96 (W.D. Wis.), dismissed without opinion, 610 F.2d 819 (7th Cir. 1979).

29. Buckley, supra note 10, 35 U.S.C. § 182.

30. See 35 U.S.C. § 182.

Timeline: The Espionage Act, Related Laws and the Press

Prepared by Eric Nelson, First Amendment Center

August 16, 2006

U.S. District Judge T. S. Ellis ordered the Justice Department "to conduct an investigation into the identity of any government employee responsible for the August 2004 disclosure to CBS News of information related to the investigation of the defendants/whether the investigation relied on information collected pursuant to Foreign Intelligence Surveillance Act."

August 10, 2006

A federal judge in Virginia stated that the Bush administration could use espionage laws to prosecute private citizens who gained access to national defense information. Steve Aftergood, the head of the Project on Government Secrecy for the Federation of American Scientists stated that "it's a momentous ruling with radical implications. A lot of people who are in the business of gathering information . . . are now going to have to grapple with the potential threat of prosecution. The dividing line has always been between leakers, who may be prosecuted, and the recipients of the leak, who have never been. Now that dividing line has been erased."

This decision is one-of-its-kind in that a court has found that citizens, other than government employees, can be charged and prosecuted for receiving and disclosing secret government information.

August 2, 2006

Senator Christopher S. "Kit" Bond, R-Mo., introduced S. 3774 "A bill to amend title 18, United States Code, to prohibit the unauthorized disclosure of classified information." The legislation is "aimed at cracking down on intelligence leaks by government employees or contractors by making it easier for the government to prosecute and punish those who make public America's sensitive intelligence programs." As the text of the legislation states, the bill is aimed at government employees and contractors as well as anyone who is, or has been, authorized to access properly classified information.

July 26, 2006

Russell Tice, a former National Security Agency (NSA) employee, is subpoenaed by a U.S. grand jury as part of an investigation into leaks of classified information. When the NSA's highly secret program of warrantless wiretapping was revealed in December 2005, Tice said publicly that he had information about "probable unlawful and unconstitutional acts" involving the NSA director, the defense secretary, and other officials as part of highly classified government operations. Tice also spoke to reporters for the *New York Times* before the newspaper published its December story disclosing the NSA program.

The subpoena says only that the grand jury is "conducting an investigation of possible violations of federal criminal laws involving the unauthorized disclosure of classified information." But it is believed to be the first public sign of the Bush administration's promised aggressive investigation into leaks about the NSA's highly secret wiretapping program.

July 18, 2006

Attorney General Alberto Gonzales tells the Senate Judiciary Committee that President Bush personally decided to block the Justice Department ethics unit from examining the role played by government lawyers in approving the National Security Agency's domestic eavesdropping program. Additionally, Gonzales is asked about his comments in a May 21 interview in which he said he had been trying to determine whether to prosecute the *New York Times* for its disclosures about the eavesdropping program. In response, Gonzales replies that, "our longstanding practice, and it remains so today, is that we pursue the leaker." He adds that the administration "hopes to work with responsible journalists and persuade them not to publish" such articles. (*New York Times*, July 19, 2006)

July 18, 2006

Senator Charles Schumer, D-N.Y., and Representative William Delahunt, D-Mass., request an inquiry into the Bush administration's apparent selective investigation into leaks of classified information to the press. In a letter to Attorney General Alberto Gonzales and Director of National Intelligence John Negroponte, Schumer and Delahunt state that while the Bush administration condemned the *New York Times* for its publication of classified information, the administration praised articles by other publications that "seem to support conclusions favorable to the administration's policies or politics." For support, Schumer and Delahunt cite eleven news reports, primarily from the *Washington Times*, containing "sensitive military and intelligence information, capabilities, methods, and sources" that the Bush administration neither condemned nor investigated.

Schumer and Delahunt: "The apparent lack of investigation into (the articles) gives the impression that the administration is unconcerned about leaks of classified information to some media sources when the revelation may have been advantageous to the administration."

July 1, 2006

Dean Baquet, editor of the *Los Angeles Times*, and Bill Keller, executive editor of the *New York Times*, cowrite an Op-Ed article defending the publication of stories about the secret Swift bank monitoring program.

Paul Steiger, managing editor of the *Wall Street Journal*, and Leonard Downie Jr., executive editor of the *Washington Post*, are asked to join the Op-Ed but both decline to take part.

June 30, 2006

A *Wall Street Journal* editorial criticizes the *New York Times* for using the *Journal* as "its ideological wingman" to deflect criticism resulting from the Swift reporting. The *Journal* editorial explains that the paper based its Swift story on "authorized" disclosures from the Treasury Department, which contacted the *Journal* with the story after it was clear that the *Times* was going to publish a similar story. (The *Journal* notes that it is a "common practice" in Washington for government officials to disclose a story that is going to become public anyway to more than one reporter.) Additionally, the *Journal* claims *Times* publisher Arthur Sulzberger Jr. does not want to win, but rather obstruct, the war on terror. Finally, the *Journal* slams the *Times* for a wide range of misdeeds, claiming the "current political clamor" is a "warning to the press about the path the *Times* is walking."

June 29, 2006

The House condemns the news media's disclosure of the government's monitoring of international banking transactions, endorsing President Bush's assertion that major newspapers acted disgracefully and undermined vital antiterrorism efforts. The GOP-crafted resolution, sponsored by Representative Michael G. Oxley, R-Ohio, is approved 227-183.

The resolution states, in part, that the House "expects the cooperation of all news media organizations in protecting the lives of Americans and the capability of the government to identify, disrupt, and capture terrorists by not disclosing classified intelligence programs such as the Terrorist Finance Tracking Program."

Further, "the disclosure of the Terrorist Finance Tracking Program has unnecessarily complicated efforts by the United States Government to prosecute the war on terror and may have placed the lives of Americans in danger both at home and in many regions of the world." It "condemns the unauthorized disclosure of classified information by those persons responsible and expresses concern that the disclosure may endanger the lives of American citizens." (*Washington Post*, June 30, 2006)

June 28, 2006

House Speaker Dennis Hastert, R-Ill., says the *New York Times* deserves a formal reprimand from Congress for publishing a report on the Treasury Department's financial-monitoring program.

Hastert: "Loose lips kill American people." (Reuters, June 28, 2006)

June 27, 2006

White House Press Secretary Tony Snow says the Bush administration's particularized criticism of the *New York Times* for its Swift story is attributable to the fact that the *Times* was "way ahead" of the *Wall Street Journal* and *Los Angeles Times* and started reporting on the story much earlier. "The other newspapers were not involved to the same extent (as the *Times*). The *Times* is really pulling the train on this one."

Snow adds that the *Times* will not lose its White House press credentials. (*Editor & Publisher*, June 27, 2006)

June 27, 2006

Representative J. D. Hayworth, R-Ariz., circulates a letter to House Speaker Dennis Hastert, R-Ill., asking House leaders to revoke the *New York Times*'s congressional press credentials.

June 27, 2006

The *New York Times* executive editor Bill Keller, in an open letter responding to critics of the *Times*'s decision to publish classified information, writes that a free press is the key check on the government's abuse of power.

June 27, 2006

Senator Pat Roberts, chairman of the Senate intelligence committee, blasts U.S. media for exposing details of highly secret intelligence programs and asks the Bush administration for a formal damage assessment. Roberts, R-Kan., asks John Negroponte, U.S. Director of National Intelligence, to report particularly on damage to Bush's domestic spying program as well as the Swift program that tracks private bank records. A Negroponte spokesman said Roberts's request was being reviewed by intelligence officials.

Roberts: "Numerous, recent unauthorized disclosures of sensitive intelligence programs have directly threatened important efforts in the war against terrorism. Whether the president's Terrorist Surveillance Program or the Department of Treasury's effort to track terrorist financing, we have been unable to persuade the media to act responsibly." (Reuters, June 27, 2006)

June 26, 2006

President Bush, Vice President Cheney, and Defense Secretary Rumsfeld denounce reports on the Swift financial data.

Bush: "[W]hat we did was fully authorized under the law. And the disclosure of this program is disgraceful. We're at war with a bunch of people who want to hurt the United States of America, and for people to leak that program, and for a newspaper to publish it, does great harm to the United States of America." (AP, June 27, 2006)

June 25, 2006

Representative Peter King, chairman of the House Homeland Security Committee, urges criminal charges against the *New York Times* for reporting on Swift, the secret financial-monitoring program used to trace terrorists. King, R-N.Y., said he would write to Attorney General Alberto Gonzales urging that the nation's chief law enforcer "begin an investigation and prosecution of the *New York Times*—the reporters, the editors and the publisher." Senator Arlen Specter, R-PA., chairman of the Senate Judiciary Committee, declines to endorse King's call for prosecution.

President Bush also condemns disclosure of the antiterrorism program, saying the disclosure of the program "makes it harder to win this war on terror." (AP, June 26, 2006)

June 23, 2006

The *New York Times*, the *Los Angeles Times*, and the *Wall Street Journal* publish articles revealing the government's classified financial-monitoring program. Using broad government subpoenas, the program allows U.S. counterterrorism analysts to obtain financial information from a vast database maintained by a company based in Belgium. It handles about eleven million financial transactions daily among 7,800 banks and other financial institutions in 200 countries.

Treasury Department officials urge the *New York Times* and the *Los Angeles Times* not to publish stories about the Swift surveillance program. The *Wall Street Journal* receives no such request.

Vice President Dick Cheney harshly criticizes the media for publishing stories regarding Swift, a financial monitoring program that Cheney deemed "absolutely essential" to the war on terror: "What I find most disturbing about these stories is the fact that some of the news media take it upon themselves to disclose vital national security programs, thereby making it more difficult for us to prevent future attacks against the American people." (*New York Times*, June 24, 2006)

June 30, 2006

In a report for Congress, the Government Accountability Office criticizes the Defense Department for sloppy management of its security classification system after finding numerous errors and problems in the department's classification activity. The report also notes that the government as a whole has no common security classification standard and no penalties for overclassification, underclassification, or failure to declassify.

May 23, 2006

Attorney General Alberto Gonzales defends the legality of the government's phone-data collection program, and softens an earlier statement regarding the possibility of prosecuting the *New York Times* reporters who first disclosed the NSA's warrantless eavesdropping program.

Gonzales: "Let me try to reassure journalists that my primary focus, quite frankly, is on the leak—on leakers who share the information with journalists." He adds that he would prefer to "try to persuade" journalists "that it would be better not to publish those kind of stories." (the *Washington Post*, May 24, 2006)

May 21, 2006

Attorney General Alberto Gonzales raises the possibility that journalists can be prosecuted under the Espionage Act for publishing classified information. "There are some statutes on the book which, if you read the language carefully, would seem to indicate that that is a possibility." (*Washington Post*, May 22, 2006)

May 18, 2006

A reporter's shield bill, entitled the "Free Flow of Information Act of 2006," is introduced by Senators Richard Lugar, R-Ind., Arlen Specter, R-Pa., Christopher Dodd, D-Conn., Lindsey Graham, R-S.C., and Charles Schumer, D-N.Y. The bill creates a qualified privilege protecting reporters from being compelled to reveal their confidential sources, subject to several exceptions, including a national security exception.

The privilege can be overcome when there is clear and convincing evidence that disclosure "(1) is necessary to prevent an act of terrorism or to prevent significant and actual harm to the national security, and (2) the value of the information that would be disclosed clearly outweighs the harm to the public interest and the free flow of information that would be caused by compelling the disclosure."

A second provision in the national security exception relates to leaks of classified information, and allows the reporter's privilege to be overcome when "(1) such unauthorized disclosure has seriously damaged the national security, (2) alternative sources of the information identifying the source have been exhausted, and (3) the harm caused by the unauthorized disclosure of properly classified Government information clearly outweighs the value to the public of the disclosed information."

May 11, 2006

USA Today reports that the NSA secretly collects phone call records of tens of millions of Americans, using data provided by AT&T, Verizon, and BellSouth. (BellSouth and Verizon deny the claims, and AT&T refuses to comment.)

Subsequently, *USA Today*, in a note to readers on June 20, 2006, backs off its assertion that BellSouth and Verizon contracted to provide telephone calling records to the NSA, acknowledging it cannot prove key elements of its May 11 story.

March 2006

Gabriel Schoenfeld, senior editor at *Commentary* magazine, proposes that the *New York Times* should be held liable under the espionage statutes for having published the Dec. 16, 2005, article revealing the existence of the Bush administration's warrantless domestic surveillance program. ("Has the *New York Times* violated the Espionage Act?" *Commentary*, March 2006)

December 16, 2005

The *New York Times* publishes an article revealing the warrantless surveillance of Americans' phone calls, carried out by the NSA.

Senior White House officials urge the *New York Times* not to publish the story. The *Times* later reports that it delayed publication of the article for a year while editors pondered the national security issues surrounding the release of the information.

November 2, 2005

The *Washington Post* publishes an article revealing CIA interrogations of al-Qaeda captives in secret prisons.

The Bush administration urges the *Post* not to publish the story. The *Post* agrees not to publish the names of the Eastern European countries involved in the covert program at the request of senior U.S. officials.

August 4, 2005

Steven J. Rosen and Keith Weissman, two former officials of a pro-Israel lobbying group, are charged with conspiring to violate the Espionage Act by allegedly disclosing classified national security information to journalists.

Lawrence A. Franklin, a U.S. Air Force Reserve colonel and former DOD analyst, who initially disclosed the classified information to Rosen and

Weissman, is later sentenced to twelve years and seven months in prison after pleading guilty to unauthorized disclosures of classified information.

January 15, 2003

Jonathan Randel, a former Drug Enforcement Administration analyst, is sentenced to a year in prison and three years of probation for theft of government property for leaking confidential but unclassified government information to the *Times* of London. Randel is convicted under 18 U.S.C. 641, which imposes criminal liability on any person who steals or knowingly converts government records "or thing[s] of value" of the United States.

May 21, 2001

The U.S. Supreme Court in *Bartnicki v. Vopper*, 532 U.S. 514 (2001), which did not directly involve the Espionage Act, notes that the press is not exempt from criminal statutes of general applicability. However, the Court declines to hold the press criminally liable for publishing information obtained in violation of federal wiretap statutes.

January 20, 2001

President Clinton pardons Samuel L. Morison, the first person ever convicted of leaking classified information to the press.

August 11, 2000

The Fourth Circuit Court of Appeals, in *United States v. Squillacote*, 221 F.3d 542 (4th Cir. 2000), determines that information "relating to the national defense," as used in the Espionage Act, is information that is "closely held" by the government. Information that is widely available to the public or information that is officially disclosed by the government does not fall under the umbrella of the Espionage Act. But if the information is closely held by the government, even if "snippets" of it have been leaked to the press and general public, it continues to be information "relating to the national defense."

Circuit Judge William B. Traxler, writing for the majority: "[A] document containing official government information relating to the national defense will not be considered available to the public (and therefore no longer national defense information) until the official information in that document is lawfully available. Thus, as the government argues, mere leaks of classified information are insufficient to prevent prosecution for the transmission of a classified document that is the official source of the leaked information."

April 1, 1988

The Fourth Circuit Court of Appeals, in *United States v. Morison*, 844 F.2d 1057 (4th Cir. 1988), affirms Samuel L. Morison's conviction of espionage for selling photographs of a Soviet nuclear-powered carrier to a British publication. The court holds that government officials can be prosecuted under the Espionage Act for leaking classified information to the press.

The Court states that §§ 793(d) and (e) are not limited to conduct that is ordinarily viewed as "classic spying," and that there is "no exemption in favor of one who leaks to the press."

The Court also determines that § 793 of the Espionage Act is not unconstitutionally vague or overbroad because the trial court's instructions properly narrowed the sweep of the statute by defining key phrases such as "national defense," "willfully," and "entitled to receive." However, Judge Dickson Phillips states that the Espionage Act's provisions are "broadly drawn" and "unwieldy and imprecise instruments for prosecuting" leakers.

Judge Harvie Wilkinson, concurring, points out that the press was not, and "probably could not," be prosecuted under the Espionage Act for publishing classified information.

Note: Morison was also convicted of violating 18 U.S.C 641 of the U.S. Criminal Code.

June 23, 1982

The Intelligence Identities Protection Act is enacted as an amendment to the National Security Act of 1947. The narrowly drawn law is designed to protect against the disclosure of information that reveals the identity of covert agents.

March 31, 1982

The Justice Department, in its report to Congress regarding the effectiveness of then-existing laws prohibiting the disclosure of classified information, states that §§ 793(d) and (e) of the Espionage Act may be violated by "unauthorized disclosures of sensitive information."

"[T]he Department of Justice has taken the position that these statutes would be violated by the unauthorized disclosure to a member of the media of classified documents or information relating to the national defense, although intent to injure the United States or benefit a foreign nation would have to be present where the disclosure is of 'information' rather than documents or other tangible materials."

March 18, 1977

Anthony A. Lapham, general counsel for the CIA, describes provisions of the Espionage Act as "vague and clumsy," stating that outside of spying, it is "extremely doubtful" that the act was intended to apply to unauthorized disclosure of information, such as the "publication of books or leaks to the press."

In a 1979 hearing before Congress, Lapham states that the ambiguity surrounding §§ 793 and 794 of the Espionage Act creates "the worst of both worlds." "On the one hand the laws stand idle and are not enforced at least in part because their meaning is so obscure, and on the other hand it is likely that the very obscurity of these laws serves to deter perfectly legitimate expression and debate by persons who must be as unsure of their liabilities as I am unsure of their obligations."

May 11, 1973

Charges against Daniel Ellsberg and Anthony Russo, who are charged under the Espionage Act for their unauthorized disclosure of the Pentagon

Papers to the press, are dismissed during the fifth month of trial on grounds of governmental misconduct.

Note: Government prosecutors relied primarily upon §§ 793(d) and (e) of the Espionage Act, as well as 18 U.S.C. 641 in their indictment of Ellsberg and Russo.

June 30, 1971

The U.S. Supreme Court in *New York Times Co. v. United States*, 403 U.S. 713 (1971), allows the continued publication of the Pentagon Papers, establishing that the press has almost absolute immunity from prepublication restraints. However, four members of the Court—Justices Byron White, Potter Stewart, Harry Blackmun, and Chief Justice Warren Burger—hold open the possibility that journalists may be criminally prosecuted under the Espionage Act for publishing or retaining defense secrets.

White, J., concurring: "It seems undeniable that a newspaper, as well as others unconnected with the Government, are vulnerable to prosecution under § 793(e) (of the Espionage Act) if they communicate or withhold the materials covered by that section."

Brennan, J., concurring, condemns injunctions "predicated upon surmise or conjecture," but nonetheless leaves open the possibility for equitable relief where "publication imperiling the safety" of the national security is at stake.

Burger, C. J., writing in dissent, expresses his belief that publishers can be prosecuted under federal laws for printing classified information.

Note: A per curiam opinion announced the judgment of the Court. Justices Black, Douglas, Brennan, Stewart, White, and Marshall each filed an individual concurring opinion. Chief Justice Burger and Justices Harlan and Blackmun wrote individual dissents.

1962

Senator John C. Stennis, D-Miss., introduces a bill to amend § 793 to make disclosures of classified information a crime, without any narrow intent requirement. The proposal is not enacted.

1957

The Government Security Commission proposes legislation criminalizing publication of classified information. The proposal, however, makes no progress in Congress and is abandoned by the Executive Branch as politically untenable.

September 24, 1951

President Harry S. Truman signs the first executive order for the protection of national security information at all federal agencies. The president's order extends classification standards that had protected military information since before World War II to include the records of all civilian agencies that have a hand in "national security" matters.

September 23, 1950

The Espionage Act is amended, creating separate sections now known as 793(d) and (e).

In response to the amendment, both the Legislative Reference Service and the Attorney General state that § 793 does not, in their view, apply to conduct ordinarily engaged in by newspapers.

Addressing concerns of some members of Congress as to the breadth of § 793(e), a provision is enacted stating that "[n]othing in this Act shall be construed to authorize, require or establish military or civilian censorship or in any way to limit or infringe upon freedom of the press or of speech as guaranteed by the Constitution of the United States and no regulation shall be promulgated hereunder having that effect." The provision is included as part of the Internal Security Act of 1950 and codified as the proviso to the Subversive Activities Act of 1950.

May 1950

Section 798 of Title 18 in the U.S. Criminal Code is enacted, criminalizing, among other things, the knowing and willful publication of "any *classified information* . . . concerning the *communication intelligence* activities of the

United States." (emphasis added) The statute does not contain any requirement that the United States be at war. Additionally, broader controls on publication are debated by Congress but are, for the most part, rejected.

The statute defines "classified information" as information "specifically designated by a United States Government Agency for limited or restricted dissemination or distribution."

The statute defines "communication intelligence" as "procedures and methods used in the interception of communications and the obtaining of information from such communications by other than the intended recipients."

At the time of its passage, § 798 is supported by the American Society of Newspaper Editors.

Note: Section 798 was enacted about four months prior to the enactment of §§ 793(d) and (e) in the Internal Security Act of 1950. However, the bill was introduced, reported, and debated in the same period as 793(d) and (e) were making their way through the legislative process.

June 28, 1948

Section 641 of Title 18 in the U.S. Criminal Code is enacted, imposing criminal liability on any person who steals or knowingly converts government records "or thing[s] of value" of the United States. The statute also criminalizes the receipt or retention of any such record or thing if the recipient intends to "convert it to his use or gain," knowing it has been stolen or converted.

The U.S. Supreme Court in *Morissette v. United States*, 342 U.S. 246 (1952), determines that conviction under § 641 cannot be sustained without criminal intent.

Although § 641 was used to prosecute both Samuel L. Morison and Jonathan Randel for unauthorized dissemination of information to the press, the statute has never been applied to punish the press for disseminating unauthorized government information to the public.

Note: Section 641 consolidates four former sections of Title 18, as adopted in 1940, which in turn were derived from two sections of the Revised Statutes.

September 18, 1947

The Central Intelligence Agency's founding statute, the National Security Act of 1947, is enacted. The act, and its subsequent amendments, shields much of the CIA's actions from public scrutiny, prohibiting "intelligence sources and methods from unauthorized disclosure."

July 20, 1946

Congress passes the Atomic Energy Act, which, together with its subsequent amendments, creates a comprehensive scheme to ensure against the disclosure of data concerning atomic weaponry and "special nuclear material." The act broadly prohibits anyone having possession of "restricted data" from communicating or disclosing such data to any person "with intent to injure the United States or with intent to secure an advantage to any foreign nation."

The legislative history does not shed light on whether Congress intends the act to be used to enjoin press publications. In the only reported opinion on the subject, a federal district court in *United States v. Progressive, Inc.*, 467 F. Supp. 990 (W.D. Wis.), in 1979 concluded that it could.

November 8, 1945

The Second Circuit in *United States v. Heine*, 151 F.2d 813 (2d Cir. 1945), determines that unless information is kept secret by the government, it cannot be considered information "relating to the national defense," as used in the Espionage Act.

August 1942

Justice Department prosecutors convene a federal grand jury to consider whether to charge the *Chicago Tribune* with violation of the Espionage Act for its publication of classified information. Ultimately, no charges are brought because the grand jury declines to indict and because military officials are unwilling to share classified information about intelligence gathering.

June 7, 1942

The *Chicago Tribune* publishes a front-page story reporting on the Battle of Midway in World War II. Without specifically publishing the fact, the *Tribune* essentially states that the United States broke Japanese naval codes and is reading the enemy's encrypted communications.

    The War Department and Justice Department contemplate criminally prosecuting the *Tribune* under the Espionage Act.

January 13, 1941

The U.S. Supreme Court in *Gorin v. United States*, 312 U.S. 19 (1941), rules that the statutory language of the Espionage Act—specifically the terms "relating to the national defense" and "connected to the national defense"— is not unconstitutionally vague. The Court determines that the term "national defense" is a "generic concept of broad connotations, referring to the military and naval establishments and the related activities of national preparedness." However, the Court narrows the statute's reach, finding that scienter or bad faith is required for conviction under §§ 793(a) and (b).

    The Court finds the bad faith standard to be bound up in the requirement that the information be "used to the injury of the United States, or to the advantage of any foreign nation."

January 12, 1938

Sections 795 and 797 of the Espionage Act are enacted, dealing with photographing and publishing photographs, pictures, drawings, or other "graphical representation(s)" of defense installations.

    Note: Sections 795 and 797 have never been the focus of judicial opinions.

December 23, 1933

President Franklin D. Roosevelt pardons those convicted under the Espionage and Sedition Acts. More than two thousand people were convicted of sedition and other violations of the Espionage Act between 1918 and 1920. Several hundred were pardoned by Presidents Warren Harding and Calvin Coolidge during the 1920s. President Roosevelt pardons every remaining person who was convicted of sedition under the federal sedition law.

June 10, 1933

Congress, in response to the publishing activities of a former State Department code-breaker, discusses and debates the problem of regulating press publication in the interest of national security. Congress eventually criminalizes the publication by federal employees of any matter originally transmitted in foreign code.

March 3, 1921

Congress repeals the Sedition Acts.

May 16, 1918

Congress passes the Sedition Act, forbidding spoken or printed criticism of the U.S. government, the Constitution, or the flag.

October 1, 1917

The Civil Liberties Bureau, a forerunner of the American Civil Liberties Union (ACLU), is formed primarily in response to passage of the Espionage Act.

June 15, 1917

Congress passes the Espionage Act of 1917, making it a crime to convey information with intent to interfere with the operation or success of the armed forces of the United States or to promote the success of its enemies.

The act criminalizes information-gathering activities, for the most part, only when performed with "intent or reason to believe that the information is to be used to the injury of the United States or to the advantage of any foreign nation."

In considering the Espionage Act of 1917, Congress narrowly rejects a provision that would have permitted the president to prohibit newspapers from publishing information concerning the national defense that the president determines might be useful to the enemy. The congressional action does not leave the law utterly without impact on publication and information-gathering, but rather makes them illegal when done with certain culpable states of mind such as "intent" or "reason to believe."

1911

Congress passes the Defense Secrets Act of 1911, a precursor to §§ 793(a) and (b), as well as portions of 793(d) and (e) and 794(a) of the Espionage Act of 1917. The statute proscribes information-gathering activities in and around military installations. It also prohibits communication of defense information to persons "not entitled to receive it."

Unlike the Espionage Act, however, the statute does not include the requirement of intent to injure the United States or advantage a foreign nation. Additionally, the Defense Secrets Act does not include the word "publishes" and the debates leading up to it do not address the idea that publication of defense information might pose a problem for national security.

The Espionage Statutes

18 U.S.C. 793, 794, 795, 797, 798 (1917)

§ 793. Gathering, transmitting or losing defense information

(a) Whoever, for the purpose of obtaining information respecting the national defense with intent or reason to believe that the information is to be used to the injury of the United States, or to the advantage of any foreign nation, goes upon, enters, flies over, or otherwise obtains information concerning any vessel, aircraft, work of defense, navy yard, naval station, submarine base, fueling station, fort, battery, torpedo station, dockyard, canal, railroad, arsenal, camp, factory, mine, telegraph, telephone, wireless, or signal station, building, office, research laboratory or station or other place connected with the national defense owned or constructed, or in progress of construction by the United States or under the control of the United States, or of any of its officers, departments, or agencies, or within the exclusive jurisdiction of the United States, or any place in which any vessel, aircraft, arms, munitions, or other materials or instruments for use in time of war are being made, prepared, repaired, stored, or are the subject of research or development, under any contract or agreement with the United States, or any department or agency thereof, or with any person on behalf of the United States, or otherwise on behalf of the United States, or any prohibited place so designated by the President by proclamation in time of war or in case of national emergency in which anything for the use of the Army, Navy, or Air Force is being prepared or constructed or stored, information as to which prohibited place the President has determined would be prejudicial to the national defense; or

(b) Whoever, for the purpose aforesaid, and with like intent or reason to believe, copies, takes, makes, or obtains, or attempts to copy, take, make, or obtain, any sketch, photograph, photographic negative, blueprint, plan, map, model, instrument, appliance, document, writing, or note of anything connected with the national defense; or

(c) Whoever, for the purpose aforesaid, receives or obtains or agrees or attempts to receive or obtain from any person, or from any source whatever, any document, writing, code book, signal book, sketch, photograph, photographic negative, blueprint, plan, map, model, instrument, appliance, or note, of anything connected with the national defense, knowing or having reason to believe, at the time he receives or obtains, or agrees or attempts to receive or obtain it, that it has been or will be obtained, taken, made, or disposed of by any person contrary to the provisions of this chapter; or

(d) Whoever, lawfully having possession of, access to, control over, or being entrusted with any document, writing, code book, signal book, sketch, photograph, photographic negative, blueprint, plan, map, model, instrument, appliance, or note relating to the national defense, or information relating to the national defense which information the possessor has reason to believe could be used to the injury of the United States or to the advantage of any foreign nation, willfully communicates, delivers, transmits or causes to be communicated, delivered, or transmitted or attempts to communicate, deliver, transmit or cause to be communicated, delivered or transmitted the same to any person not entitled to receive it, or willfully retains the same and fails to deliver it on demand to the officer or employee of the United States entitled to receive it; or

(e) Whoever having unauthorized possession of, access to, or control over any document, writing, code book, signal book, sketch, photograph, photographic negative, blueprint, plan, map, model, instrument, appliance, or note relating to the national defense, or information relating to the national defense which information the possessor has reason to believe could be used to the injury of the United States or to the advantage of any foreign nation, willfully communicates, delivers, transmits or causes to be communicated, delivered, or transmitted, or attempts to communicate, deliver, transmit or cause to be communicated, delivered, or transmitted the same to any person not entitled to receive it, or willfully retains the same and fails to deliver it to the officer or employee of the United States entitled to receive it; or

(f) Whoever, being entrusted with or having lawful possession or control of any document, writing, code book, signal book, sketch, photograph, photographic negative, blueprint, plan, map, model, instrument, appliance, note, or information, relating to the national defense,

> (1) through gross negligence permits the same to be removed from its proper place of custody or delivered to anyone in violation of his trust, or to be lost, stolen, abstracted, or destroyed, or
> (2) having knowledge that the same has been illegally removed from its proper place of custody or delivered to anyone in violation of its trust, or lost, or stolen, abstracted, or destroyed, and fails to make prompt report of such loss, theft, abstraction, or destruction to his superior officer—

Shall be fined under this title or imprisoned not more than ten years, or both.

(g) If two or more persons conspire to violate any of the foregoing provisions of this section, and one or more of such persons do any act to effect the object of the conspiracy, each of the parties to such conspiracy shall be subject to the punishment provided for the offense which is the object of such conspiracy.

(h)

> (1) Any person convicted of a violation of this section shall forfeit to the United States, irrespective of any provision of State law, any property constituting, or derived from, any proceeds the person obtained, directly or indirectly, from any foreign government, or any faction or party or military or naval force within a foreign country, whether recognized

or unrecognized by the United States, as the result of such violation. For the purposes of this subsection, the term "State" includes a State of the United States, the District of Columbia, and any commonwealth, territory, or possession of the United States.

(2) The court, in imposing sentence on a defendant for a conviction of a violation of this section, shall order that the defendant forfeit to the United States all property described in paragraph (1) of this subsection.

(3) The provisions of subsections (b), (c), and (e) through (p) of section 413 of the Comprehensive Drug Abuse Prevention and Control Act of 1970 (21 U.S.C. 853 (b), (c), and (e)–(p)) shall apply to—

(A) property subject to forfeiture under this subsection;

(B) any seizure or disposition of such property; and

(C) any administrative or judicial proceeding in relation to such property, if not inconsistent with this subsection.

(4) Notwithstanding section 524 (c) of title 28, there shall be deposited in the Crime Victims Fund in the Treasury all amounts from the forfeiture of property under this subsection remaining after the payment of expenses for forfeiture and sale authorized by law.

§ 794. Gathering or delivering defense information to aid foreign government

(a) Whoever, with intent or reason to believe that it is to be used to the injury of the United States or to the advantage of a foreign nation, communicates, delivers, or transmits, or attempts to communicate, deliver, or transmit, to any foreign government, or to any faction or party or military or naval force within a foreign country, whether recognized or unrecognized by the United States, or to any representative, officer, agent, employee, subject, or citizen thereof, either directly or indirectly, any document, writing, code book, signal book, sketch, photograph, photographic negative, blueprint, plan, map, model, note, instrument, appliance, or information relating to the national defense, shall be punished by death or by imprisonment for any term of years or for life, except that the sentence of death shall not be imposed unless the jury or, if there is no jury, the court, further finds that the offense resulted in the identification by a foreign power (as defined in section 101(a) of the Foreign Intelligence Surveillance Act of 1978) of an individual acting as an agent of the United States and consequently in the death of that individual, or directly concerned nuclear weaponry, military spacecraft or satellites, early warning systems, or other means of defense or retaliation against large-scale attack; war plans; communications intelligence or cryptographic information; or any other major weapons system or major element of defense strategy.

(b) Whoever, in time of war, with intent that the same shall be communicated to the enemy, collects, records, publishes, or communicates, or attempts to elicit any information with respect to the movement, numbers, description, condition, or disposition of any of the Armed Forces, ships, aircraft, or war materials of the United States, or with respect to the plans or conduct, or supposed plans or conduct of any naval or military operations, or with respect to any works or measures undertaken for or connected with, or intended for the fortification or defense of any place, or any other information relating to the public defense, which might be useful to the enemy, shall be punished by death or by imprisonment for any term of years or for life.

(c) If two or more persons conspire to violate this section, and one or more of such persons do any act to effect the object of the conspiracy, each of the parties to such conspiracy shall be subject to the punishment provided for the offense which is the object of such conspiracy.

(d)
> (1) Any person convicted of a violation of this section shall forfeit to the United States irrespective of any provision of State law—
>> (A) any property constituting, or derived from, any proceeds the person obtained, directly or indirectly, as the result of such violation, and
>> (B) any of the person's property used, or intended to be used, in any manner or part, to commit, or to facilitate the commission of, such violation.
>> For the purposes of this subsection, the term "State" includes a State of the United States, the District of Columbia, and any commonwealth, territory, or possession of the United States.

(2) The court, in imposing sentence on a defendant for a conviction of a violation of this section, shall order that the defendant forfeit to the United States all property described in paragraph (1) of this subsection. (3) The provisions of subsections (b), (c) and (e) through (p) of section 413 of the Comprehensive Drug Abuse Prevention and Control Act of 1970 (21 U.S.C. 853 (b), (c), and (e)–(p)) shall apply to—

(A) property subject to forfeiture under this subsection;

(B) any seizure or disposition of such property; and

(C) any administrative or judicial proceeding in relation to such property, if not inconsistent with this subsection.

(4) Notwithstanding section 524 (c) of title 28, there shall be deposited in the Crime Victims Fund in the Treasury all amounts from the forfeiture of property under this subsection remaining after the payment of expenses for forfeiture and sale authorized by law.

§ 795. Photographing and sketching defense installations

(a) Whenever, in the interests of national defense, the President defines certain vital military and naval installations or equipment as requiring protection against the general dissemination of information relative thereto, it shall be unlawful to make any photograph, sketch, picture, drawing, map, or graphical representation of such vital military and naval installations or equipment without first obtaining permission of the commanding officer of the military or naval post, camp, or station, or naval vessels, military and naval aircraft, and any separate military or naval command concerned, or higher authority, and promptly submitting the product obtained to such commanding officer or higher authority for censorship or such other action as he may deem necessary.

(b) Whoever violates this section shall be fined under this title or imprisoned not more than one year, or both.

§ 797. Publication and sale of photographs of defense installations

On and after thirty days from the date upon which the President defines any vital military or naval installation or equipment as being within the category contemplated under section 795 of this title, whoever reproduces, publishes, sells, or gives away any photograph, sketch, picture, drawing, map, or graphical representation of the vital military or naval installations or equipment so defined, without first obtaining permission of the commanding officer of the military or naval post, camp, or station concerned, or higher authority, unless such photograph, sketch, picture, drawing, map, or graphical representation has clearly indicated thereon that it has been censored by the proper military or naval authority, shall be fined under this title or imprisoned not more than one year, or both.

§ 798. Disclosure of classified information

(a) Whoever knowingly and willfully communicates, furnishes, transmits, or otherwise makes available to an unauthorized person, or publishes, or uses in any manner prejudicial to the safety or interest of the United States or for the benefit of any foreign government to the detriment of the United States any classified information—

(1) concerning the nature, preparation, or use of any code, cipher, or cryptographic system of the United States or any foreign government; or

(2) concerning the design, construction, use, maintenance, or repair of any device, apparatus, or appliance used or prepared or planned for use by the United States or any foreign government for cryptographic or communication intelligence purposes; or

(3) concerning the communication intelligence activities of the United States or any foreign government; or

(4) obtained by the processes of communication intelligence from the communications of any foreign government, knowing the same to have been obtained by such processes—

Shall be fined under this title or imprisoned not more than ten years, or both.

(b) As used in subsection (a) of this section—

The term "classified information" means information which, at the time of a violation of this section, is, for reasons of national security, specifically designated by a United States Government Agency for limited or restricted dissemination or distribution;

The terms "code," "cipher," and "cryptographic system" include in their meanings, in addition to their usual meanings, any method of secret writing and any mechanical or electrical device or method used for the purpose of disguising or concealing the contents, significance, or meanings of communications;

The term "foreign government" includes in its meaning any person or persons acting or purporting to act for or on behalf of any faction, party, department, agency, bureau, or military force of or within a foreign country, or for or on behalf of any government or any person or persons purporting to act as a government within a foreign country, whether or not such government is recognized by the United States;

The term "communication intelligence" means all procedures and methods used in the interception of communications and the obtaining of information from such communications by other than the intended recipients;

The term "unauthorized person" means any person who, or agency which, is not authorized to receive information of the categories set forth in subsection (a) of this section, by the President, or by the head of a department or agency of the United States Government which is expressly designated by the President to engage in communication intelligence activities for the United States.

(c) Nothing in this section shall prohibit the furnishing, upon lawful demand, of information to any regularly constituted committee of the Senate or House of Representatives of the United States of America, or joint committee thereof.

(d)

    (1) Any person convicted of a violation of this section shall forfeit to the United States irrespective of any provision of State law—

(A) any property constituting, or derived from, any proceeds the person obtained, directly or indirectly, as the result of such violation; and

(B) any of the person's property used, or intended to be used, in any manner or part, to commit, or to facilitate the commission of, such violation.

(2) The court, in imposing sentence on a defendant for a conviction of a violation of this section, shall order that the defendant forfeit to the United States all property described in paragraph (1).

(3) Except as provided in paragraph (4), the provisions of subsections (b), (c), and (e) through (p) of section 413 of the Comprehensive Drug Abuse Prevention and Control Act of 1970 (21 U.S.C. 853 (b), (c), and (e)–(p)), shall apply to—

(A) property subject to forfeiture under this subsection;

(B) any seizure or disposition of such property; and

(C) any administrative or judicial proceeding in relation to such property, if not inconsistent with this subsection.

(4) Notwithstanding section 524 (c) of title 28, there shall be deposited in the Crime Victims Fund established under section 1402 of the Victims of Crime Act of 1984 (42 U.S.C. 10601) all amounts from the forfeiture of property under this subsection remaining after the payment of expenses for forfeiture and sale authorized by law.

(5) As used in this subsection, the term "State" means any State of the United States, the District of Columbia, the Commonwealth of Puerto Rico, and any territory or possession of the United States.

The Pentagon Papers Case

New York Times Co. v. United States;
United States v. Washington Post Co.
403 U.S. 713 (1971)

[On June 12-14, 1971, the *New York Times* and, on June 18, the *Washington Post* published excerpts from a top secret Defense Department study of the Vietnam War. The study, which was commissioned by Robert McNamara in 1967, filled forty-seven volumes and reviewed in great detail the formulation of U.S. policy toward Indochina, including military operations and secret diplomatic negotiations. The newspapers obtained the study, known popularly as the Pentagon Papers, from Daniel Ellsberg, a former Pentagon official. The government filed suit in federal district courts in New York and Washington, D.C., seeking to enjoin further publication of the materials, claiming that such publication would interfere with national security and would lead to the death of soldiers, the undermining of our alliances, the inability of our diplomats to negotiate, and the prolongation of the war. Between June 15 and June 23, the cases worked their way through the federal courts, and on June 26, the Supreme Court heard argument. On June 30, the Court issued its decision. Restraining orders remained in effect throughout the Court's deliberations.]

PER CURIAM.

We granted certiorari in these cases in which the United States seeks to enjoin the *New York Times* and the *Washington Post* from publishing the contents of a classified study entitled "History of U.S. Decision-Making Process on Viet Nam Policy."

"Any system of prior restraints of expression comes to this Court bearing a heavy presumption against its constitutional validity." [The] Government "thus carries a heavy burden of showing justification for the imposition of such a restraint." [The] District Court for the Southern District of New York in the *New York Times* case and the District Court for the District of Columbia and the Court of Appeals for the District of Columbia Circuit in the *Washington Post* case held that the Government had not met that burden. We agree.

The judgment of the Court of Appeals for the District of Columbia Circuit is therefore affirmed. The order of the Court of Appeals for the Second Circuit is reversed and the case is remanded with directions to enter a judgment affirming the judgment of the District Court for the Southern District of New York. The stays entered June 25, 1971, by the Court are vacated. The judgments shall issue forthwith.

So ordered.

MR. JUSTICE BLACK, with whom MR. JUSTICE DOUGLAS joins, concurring. . . .

[Every] moment's continuance of the injunctions against these newspapers amounts to a flagrant, indefensible, and continuing violation of the First Amendment. [For] the first time in the 182 years since the founding of the Republic, the federal courts are asked to hold that the First Amendment does not mean what it says, but rather means that the Government can halt the publication of current news of vital importance to the people of this country. . . .

In the First Amendment the Founding Fathers gave the free press the protection it must have to fulfill its essential role in our democracy. The press was to serve the governed, not the governors. The Government's power to censor the press was abolished so that the press would remain forever free to censure the Government. The press was protected so that it could bare the secrets of government and inform the people. Only a free and unrestrained press can effectively expose deception in government. . . .

[We] are asked to hold that despite the First Amendment's emphatic command, the Executive Branch, the Congress, and the Judiciary can make laws enjoining publication of current news and abridging freedom of the press in the name of "national security." . . .

The word "security" is a broad, vague generality whose contours should not be invoked to abrogate the fundamental law embodied in the First Amendment. The guarding of military and diplomatic secrets at the expense of informed representative government provides no real security for our Republic.

MR. JUSTICE DOUGLAS, with whom MR. JUSTICE BLACK joins, concurring. . . .

These disclosures may have a serious impact. But that is no basis for sanctioning a previous restraint on the press. [The] dominant purpose of the First Amendment was to prohibit the widespread practice of governmental suppression of embarrassing information. It is common knowledge that the First Amendment was adopted against the widespread use of the common law of seditious libel to punish the dissemination of material that is embarrassing to the powers-that-be. [A] debate of large proportions goes on in the Nation over our posture in Vietnam. That debate antedated the disclosure of the contents of the present documents. The latter are highly relevant to the debate in progress.

Secrecy in government is fundamentally anti-democratic, perpetuating bureaucratic errors. Open debate and discussion of public issues are vital to our national health. On public questions there should be "uninhibited, robust, and wide-open" debate. . . .

The stays in these cases that have been in effect for more than a week constitute a flouting of the principles of the First Amendment. . . .

MR. JUSTICE BRENNAN, concurring.

The error that has pervaded these cases from the outset was the granting of any injunctive relief whatsoever, interim or otherwise. The entire thrust of the Government's claim throughout these cases has been that publication of the material sought to be enjoined "could," or "might," or "may" prejudice the national interest in various ways. But the First Amendment tolerates absolutely no prior judicial restraints of the press predicated upon surmise or conjecture that untoward consequences may result.* Our cases, it is true, have indicated that there is a single, extremely narrow class of cases in which the First Amendment's ban on prior judicial restraint may be overridden. Our cases have thus far indicated that such cases may arise only when the Nation "is at war," [*Schenck*], during which times "[n]o one would question but that a government might prevent actual obstruction to its recruiting service or the publication of the sailing dates of transports or the number and location of troops." *Near v. Minnesota*, [chapter III, section B infra]. Even if the present world situation were assumed to be tantamount to a time of war, or if the power of presently available armaments would justify even in peacetime the suppression of information that would set in motion a nuclear holocaust, in neither of these actions has the Government presented or even alleged that publication of items from or based upon the material at issue would cause the happening of an event of that nature. "[T]he chief purpose of [the First Amendment's] guaranty [is]to prevent previous restraints upon publication." [*Near.*] Thus, only governmental allegation and proof that publication must inevitably, directly, and immediately cause the occurrence of an event kindred to imperiling the safety of a transport already at sea can support even the issuance of an interim restraining order. [Every] restraint issued in this case, whatever its form, has violated the First Amendment—and not less so because that restraint was justified as necessary to afford the courts an opportunity to examine the claim more thoroughly. Unless and until the Government has clearly made out its case, the First Amendment commands that no injunction may issue.

MR. JUSTICE STEWART, with whom MR. JUSTICE WHITE joins, concurring.

In the governmental structure created by our Constitution, the Executive is endowed with enormous power in the two related areas of national

---

Freedman v. Maryland, 380 U.S. 51 (1965), and similar cases regarding temporary restraints of allegedly obscene materials are not in point. For those cases rest upon the proposition that "obscenity is not protected by the freedoms of speech and press." [Here] there is no question but that the material sought to be suppressed is within the protection of the First Amendment; the only question is whether, notwithstanding that fact, its publication may be enjoined for a time because of the presence of an overwhelming national interest.

defense and international relations. This power, largely unchecked by the Legislative and Judicial branches, has been pressed to the very hilt since the advent of the nuclear missile age....

In the absence of the governmental checks and balances present in other areas of our national life, the only effective restraint upon executive policy and power in the areas of national defense and international affairs may lie in an enlightened citizenry—in an informed and critical public opinion which alone can here protect the values of democratic government....

Yet it is elementary that the successful conduct of international diplomacy and the maintenance of an effective national defense require both confidentiality and secrecy. Other nations can hardly deal with this Nation in an atmosphere of mutual trust unless they can be assured that their confidences will be kept. And within our own executive departments, the development of considered and intelligent international policies would be impossible if those charged with their formulation could not communicate with each other freely, frankly, and in confidence. In the area of basic national defense the frequent need for absolute secrecy is, of course, self-evident.

I think there can be but one answer to this dilemma, if dilemma it be. The responsibility must be where the power is. If the Constitution gives the Executive a large degree of unshared power in the conduct of foreign affairs and the maintenance of our national defense, then under the Constitution the Executive must have the largely unshared duty to determine and preserve the degree of internal security necessary to exercise that power successfully. [It] is clear to me that it is the constitutional duty of the Executive—as a matter of sovereign prerogative and not as a matter of law as the courts know law—through the promulgation and enforcement of executive regulations, to protect the confidentiality necessary to carry out its responsibilities in the fields of international relations and national defense.

This is not to say that Congress and the courts have no role to play. Undoubtedly Congress has the power to enact specific and appropriate criminal laws to protect government property and preserve government secrets....

But in the cases before us we are asked neither to construe specific regulations nor to apply specific laws. We are asked, instead, to perform a function that the Constitution gave to the Executive, not the Judiciary. We are asked, quite simply, to prevent the publication by two newspapers of material that the Executive Branch insists should not, in the national interest, be published. I am convinced that the Executive is correct with respect to some of the documents involved. But I cannot say that disclosure of any of them will surely result in direct, immediate, and irreparable damage to our Nation or its people. That being so, there can under the First Amendment be but one judicial resolution of the issues before us. I join the judgments of the Court.

MR. JUSTICE WHITE, with whom MR. JUSTICE STEWART joins, concurring.

I concur in today's judgments, but only because of the concededly extraordinary protection against prior restraints enjoyed by the press under our constitutional system. I do not say that in no circumstances would the First Amendment permit an injunction against publishing information about government plans or operations. Nor, after examining the materials the Government characterizes as the most sensitive and destructive, can I deny that revelation of these documents will do substantial damage to public interests. Indeed, I am confident that their disclosure will have that result. But I nevertheless agree that the United States has not satisfied the very heavy burden that it must meet to warrant an injunction against publication in these cases, at least in the absence of express and appropriately limited congressional authorization for prior restraints in circumstances such as these.

The Government's position is simply stated: The responsibility of the Executive for the conduct of the foreign affairs and for the security of the Nation is so basic that the President is entitled to an injunction against publication of a newspaper story whenever he can convince a court that the information to be revealed threatens "grave and irreparable" injury to the public interest; and the injunction should issue whether or not the material to be published is classified, whether or not publication would be lawful under relevant criminal statutes enacted by Congress, and regardless of the circumstances by which the newspaper came into possession of the information.

At least in the absence of legislation by Congress, based on its own investigations and findings, I am quite unable to agree that the inherent powers of the Executive and the courts reach so far as to authorize remedies having such sweeping potential for inhibiting publications by the press. . . .

[Prior] restraints require an unusually heavy justification under the First Amendment; but failure by the Government to justify prior restraints does not measure its constitutional entitlement to a conviction for criminal publication. That the Government mistakenly chose to proceed by injunction does not mean that it could not successfully proceed in another way. . . .

The Criminal Code contains numerous provisions potentially relevant to these cases. [Section] 793(e)[8] makes it a criminal act for any unauthorized possessor of a document "relating to the national defense" either (1) willfully to communicate or cause to be communicated that document to any person not entitled to receive it or (2) willfully to retain the document and fail to deliver it to an officer of the United States entitled to receive it. . . .

It is thus clear that Congress has addressed itself to the problems of protecting the security of the country and the national defense from unauthorized disclosure of potentially damaging information. [It] has not, however, authorized the injunctive remedy against threatened publication. It has apparently been satisfied to rely on criminal sanctions and their deterrent effect on the responsible as well as the irresponsible press. I am not, of course, saying that either of these newspapers has yet committed a crime or that either would commit a crime if it published all the material now in its possession. That matter must await resolution in the context of a criminal proceeding if one is instituted by the United States. . . .

---

8. Section 793(e) of 18 U.S.C. provides that:

(e) Whoever having unauthorized possession of, access to, or control over any document, writing, code book, signal book, sketch, photograph, photographic negative, blueprint, plan, map, model, instrument, appliance, or note relating to the national defense, or information relating to the national defense which information the possessor has reason to believe could be used to the injury of the United States or to the advantage of any foreign nation, willfully communicates, delivers, transmits or causes to be communicated, delivered, or transmitted, or attempts to communicate, deliver, transmit or cause to be communicated, delivered, or transmitted the same to any person not entitled to receive it, or willfully retains the same and fails to deliver it to the officer or employee of the United States entitled to receive it; is guilty of an offense punishable by 10 years in prison, a $10,000 fine, or both.

MR. JUSTICE MARSHALL, concurring.

I believe the ultimate issue in these cases [is] whether this Court or the Congress has the power to make law. . . .

The problem here is whether in these particular cases the Executive Branch has authority to invoke the equity jurisdiction of the courts to protect what it believes to be the national interest. [I]n some situations it may be that under whatever inherent powers the Government may have, as well as the implicit authority derived from the President's mandate to conduct foreign affairs and to act as Commander in Chief, there is a basis for the invocation of the equity jurisdiction of this Court as an aid to prevent the publication of material damaging to "national security," however that term may be defined.

It would, however, be utterly inconsistent with the concept of separation of powers for this Court to use its power of contempt to prevent behavior that Congress has specifically declined to prohibit. [The] Constitution provides that Congress shall make laws, the President execute laws, and courts interpret laws. [It] did not provide for government by injunction in which the courts and the Executive Branch can "make law" without regard to the action of Congress. [It] is clear that Congress has specifically rejected passing legislation that would have clearly given the President the power he seeks here and made the current activity of the newspapers unlawful. When Congress specifically declines to make conduct unlawful it is not for this Court to redecide those issues—to overrule Congress. . . .

MR. CHIEF JUSTICE BURGER, dissenting.

[In] these cases, the imperative of a free and unfettered press comes into collision with another imperative, the effective functioning of a complex modern government and specifically the effective exercise of certain constitutional powers of the Executive. Only those who view the First Amendment as an absolute in all circumstances—a view I respect, but reject—can find such cases as these to be simple or easy.

These cases are not simple for another and more immediate reason. We do not know the facts of the cases. No District Judge knew all the facts. No Court of Appeals judge knew all the facts. No member of this Court knows all the facts. . . .

I suggest we are in this posture because these cases have been conducted in unseemly haste. [It] seems reasonably clear now that the haste precluded reasonable and deliberate judicial treatment of these cases and was not warranted. The precipitate action of this Court aborting trials not yet completed is not the kind of judicial conduct that ought to attend the disposition of a great issue. . . .

It is not disputed that the *Times* has had unauthorized possession of the documents for three to four months, during which it has had its expert analysts studying them, presumably digesting them and preparing the material for publication. During all of this time, the *Times*, presumably in its capacity as trustee of the public's "right to know," has held up publication for purposes it considered proper and thus public knowledge was delayed. No doubt this was for a good reason; the analysis of 7,000 pages of complex material drawn from a vastly greater volume of material would inevitably take time and the writing of good news stories takes time. But why should the United States Government, from whom this information was illegally acquired by someone, along with all the counsel, trial judges, and appellate judges be placed under needless pressure? After these months of deferral, the alleged "right to know" has somehow and suddenly become a right that must be vindicated instanter. . . .

I would affirm the Court of Appeals for the Second Circuit and allow the District Court to complete the trial aborted by our grant of certiorari, meanwhile preserving the status quo in the *Post* case. I would direct that the District Court on remand give priority to the *Times* case to the exclusion of all other business of that court but I would not set arbitrary deadlines. . . .

We all crave speedier judicial processes but when judges are pressured as in these cases the result is a parody of the judicial function.

MR. JUSTICE HARLAN, with whom THE CHIEF JUSTICE and MR. JUSTICE BLACKMUN join, dissenting. . . .

With all respect, I consider that the Court has been almost irresponsibly feverish in dealing with these cases.

Both the Court of Appeals for the Second Circuit and the Court of Appeals for the District of Columbia Circuit rendered judgment on June 23. The *New York Times*'s petition for certiorari, its motion for accelerated consideration thereof, and its application for interim relief were filed in this Court on June 24 at about 11 a.m. The application of the United States

for interim relief in the *Post* case was also filed here on June 24 at about
7:15 p.m. This Court's order setting a hearing before us on June 26 at 11
a.m., a course which I joined only to avoid the possibility of even more
peremptory action by the Court, was issued less than 24 hours before. The
record in the *Post* case was filed with the Clerk shortly before 1 p.m. on
June 25; the record in the *Times* case did not arrive until seven or eight
o'clock that same night. The briefs of the parties were received less than
two hours before argument on June 26.

This frenzied train of events took place in the name of the presumption
against prior restraints created by the First Amendment. Due regard for the
extraordinarily important and difficult questions involved in these litiga-
tions should have led the Court to shun such a precipitate timetable. . . .

Forced as I am to reach the merits of these cases, I dissent from the
opinion and judgments of the Court. [It] is plain to me that the scope of
the judicial function in passing upon the activities of the Executive Branch
of the Government in the field of foreign affairs is very narrowly restricted.
This view is, I think, dictated by the concept of separation of powers upon
which our constitutional system rests. . . .

The power to evaluate the "pernicious influence" of premature disclosure is not, however, lodged in the Executive alone. I agree that, in perfor-
mance of its duty to protect the values of the First Amendment against
political pressures, the judiciary must review the initial Executive determination to the point of satisfying itself that the subject matter of the dispute
does lie within the proper compass of the President's foreign relations
power. Constitutional considerations forbid "a complete abandonment of
judicial control." [Moreover], the judiciary may properly insist that the
determination that disclosure of the subject matter would irreparably
impair the national security be made by the head of the Executive Department concerned—here the Secretary of State or the Secretary of Defense—
after actual personal consideration by that officer. . . .

But in my judgment the judiciary may not properly go beyond these
two inquiries and redetermine for itself the probable impact of disclosure
on the national security.

[T]he very nature of executive decisions as to foreign policy is political, not judicial. Such decisions are wholly confided by our Constitution to

the political departments of the government, Executive and Legislative. They are delicate, complex, and involve large elements of prophecy. They are and should be undertaken only by those directly responsible to the people whose welfare they advance or imperil. They are decisions of a kind for which the Judiciary has neither aptitude, facilities nor responsibility and which has long been held to belong in the domain of political power not subject to judicial intrusion or inquiry.

Chicago & Southern Air Lines v. Waterman Steamship Corp., 333 U.S. 103, 111 (1948) (Jackson, J.).

Even if there is some room for the judiciary to override the executive determination, it is plain that the scope of review must be exceedingly narrow. I can see no indication in the opinions of either the District Court or the Court of Appeals in the *Post* litigation that the conclusions of the Executive were given even the deference owing to an administrative agency, much less that owing to a co-equal branch of the Government operating within the field of its constitutional prerogative. . . .

Pending further hearings in each case conducted under the appropriate ground rules, I would continue the restraints on publication. I cannot believe that the doctrine prohibiting prior restraints reaches to the point of preventing courts from maintaining the status quo long enough to act responsibly in matters of such national importance as those involved here.

Mr. Justice Blackmun, dissenting.

The First Amendment, after all, is only one part of an entire Constitution. Article II of the great document vests in the Executive Branch primary power over the conduct of foreign affairs and places in that branch the responsibility for the Nation's safety. Each provision of the Constitution is important, and I cannot subscribe to a doctrine of unlimited absolutism for the First Amendment at the cost of downgrading other provisions. First Amendment absolutism has never commanded a majority of this Court. [What] is needed here is a weighing, upon properly developed standards, of the broad right of the press to print and of the very narrow right of the Government to prevent. Such standards are not yet developed. The parties here are in disagreement as to what those standards should be. But even the newspapers concede that there are situations where restraint is in order and is constitutional. . . .

I therefore would remand these cases to be developed expeditiously, of course, but on a schedule permitting the orderly presentation of evidence from both sides. . . . The Court, however, decides the cases today the other way. I therefore add one final comment.

I strongly urge, and sincerely hope, that these two newspapers will be fully aware of their ultimate responsibilities to the United States of America. Judge Wilkey, dissenting in the District of Columbia case [concluded] that there were a number of examples of documents that, if in the possession of the *Post*, and if published, "could clearly result in great harm to the nation," and he defined "harm" to mean "the death of soldiers, the destruction of alliances, the greatly increased difficulty of negotiation with our enemies, the inability of our diplomats to negotiate. . . ." I, for one, have now been able to give at least some cursory study not only to the affidavits, but to the material itself. I regret to say that from this examination I fear that Judge Wilkey's statements have possible foundation. I therefore share his concern. I hope that damage has not already been done. If, however, damage has been done, and if, with the Court's action today, these newspapers proceed to publish the critical documents and there results therefrom "the death of soldiers, the destruction of alliances, the greatly increased difficulty of negotiations with our enemies, the inability of our diplomats to negotiate," to which list I might add the factors of prolongation of the war and of further delay in the freeing of United States prisoners, then the Nation's people will know where the responsibility for these sad consequences rests.

Selected Bibliography

Prepared by Eric Nelson and Rebecca Schwartz, First Amendment Center

Court Cases

Abrams v. United States, 250 U.S. 616 (1919).

Bartnicki v. Vopper, 532 U.S. 514 (2001).

Debs v. United States, 249 U.S. 211 (1919).

Dennis v. United States, 341 U.S. 494 (1951) [Smith Act].

Dubin v. United States, 176 Ct. Cl. 702 (Ct. Cl. 1966), cert. denied, 386 U.S. 956 (1967).

Frohwerk v. United States, 249 U.S. 204 (1919).

Gorin v. United States, 312 U.S. 19 (1941).

Gros v. United States, 138 F.2d 261 (9th Cir. 1943).

New York Times Co. v. United States, 403 U.S. 713 (1971) [prior restraint].

Scarbeck v. United States, 223 F. Supp. 900 (D.C. Cir. 1963) [Internal Security Act].

Schaefer v. United States, 251 U.S. 466 (1920).

Schenck v. United States, 249 U.S. 47 (1919).

Slack v. United States, 203 F.2d 152 (6th Cir. 1953).

United States ex rel. Milwaukee Social Democrat Publishing Co. v. Burleson, 255 U.S. 407 (1921).

United States v. Coplon, 88 F. Supp. 910 (S.D.N.Y. 1949).
United States v. Dedayan, 584 F.2d 36 (4th Cir. 1978).
United States v. Heine, 151 F.2d 813 (2d Cir. 1945, per L. Hand, J.), cert. denied, 328 U.S. 833 (1946).
United States v. Lindh, 212 F. Supp. 2d 541 (E.D. Va. 2002).
United States v. McGuinness, 33 M.J. 781 (N.M.C.M.R. 1991).
United States v. Morison, 844 F.2d 1057 (4th Cir. 1988).
United States v. Pelton, 835 F.2d 1067 (4th Cir. 1987).
United States v. Rosenberg, 195 F.2d 583 (2d Cir. 1952), cert. denied, 344 U.S. 889 (1952).
United States v. Squillacote, 221 F.3d 542 (4th Cir. 2000).
United States v. Troung Dinh Hung, 629 F.2d 908 (4th Cir. 1980).

Relevant Statutes

Atomic Energy Act. 42 U.S.C. §§ 2011-2259 (1954).
Criminal Code: Diplomatic codes and correspondence. 18 U.S.C. § 952 (1948).
Criminal Code: Theft or conversion of government property. 18 U.S.C. § 641 (2004).
Defense Secrets Act. 36 Stat. § 1804 (1911).
Economic Espionage Act of 1996. 18 U.S.C. § 1831 (1996).
Espionage Act of 1917. 18 U.S.C. §§ 793, 794, 795, 797, 798 (1917).
Foreign Intelligence Surveillance Act. 50 U.S.C. § 1801 (2006).
Industrial Espionage Act. 18 U.S.C. § 90 (1996).
Intelligence Identities Protection Act. 50 U.S.C. §§ 421-426 (1982).
Internal Security Act (also known as the McCarran-Wood Act). 50 U.S.C. § 781 (1950).
Sedition Act (1918) (an amendment to the Espionage Act of 1917; repealed in 1921).
Smith Act. 18 U.S.C. § 2385 (1970).
USA Patriot Act. PL 107-56 (2006).

Books

Chaffee, Zechariah Jr. (1948). *Free Speech in the United States*. Cambridge, MA: Harvard University Press.
Dickson, Del (2001). *The Supreme Court in Conference (1940-1985): The Private Discussions behind Nearly 300 Supreme Court Decisions*, 369-372. New York: Oxford University Press.

Dulles, A. (1963). *The Craft of Intelligence*. New York: Harper and Row.

Emerson, Thomas (1970). *The System of Freedom of Expression*. New York: Random House.

Kohn, Stephen J. (1994). *American Political Prisoners: Prosecutions under the Espionage and Seditions Acts*. Westport, CT: Praeger.

Linsky, M. (1986). *Impact: How the Press Affects Federal Policy Making*. New York: W. W. Norton & Company, Inc.

Murphy, Paul L. (1979). *World War I and the Origins of Civil Liberties in the United States*. New York: W. W. Norton & Company, Inc.

Murray, Robert K. (1955). *Red Scare: A Study in National Hysteria, 1919-1920*. Minneapolis: University of Minnesota Press.

Perisco, Joseph E. (2001). *Roosevelt's Secret War: FDR and World War II Espionage*. Toronto: Random House.

Polenberg, Richard (1987). *Fighting Faiths: The Abrams Case, Free Speech, and the Supreme Court*. New York: Viking.

Prados, John, and Porter, Margaret Pratt (editors). (2005). *Inside the Pentagon Papers*. Lawrence: University Press of Kansas.

Rabban, David M. (1997). *Free Speech in Its Forgotten Years*. Cambridge: Cambridge University Press.

Redish, Martin (2005). *The Logic of Persecution: Free Speech & the McCarthy Era*. Palo Alto, CA: Stanford University Press.

Risen, James (2006). *State of War: The Secret History of the CIA and the Bush Administration*. New York: Free Press.

Rudenstine, David (1996). *The Day the Presses Stopped: A History of the Pentagon Papers Case*, 61-62, 105-6, 108, 128-29, 309-10, 311. University of California Press.

Schauer, Frederick (1982). *Free Speech: A Philosophical Enquiry*, 197-200. Cambridge: Cambridge University Press.

Smith, Jeffrey A. (1999). *War Press and Freedom: The Problem of Prerogative Power*. New York: Oxford University Press.

Smolla, Rodney A. (1994). *Smolla and Nimmer on Freedom of Speech: A Treatise on the Theory of the First Amendment*, § 8.03(2)(c)(i)-(iv). Matthew Bender.

Stone, Geoffrey R. (2004). *Perilous Times: Free Speech in Wartime*. New York: W. W. Norton & Company, Inc.

Turner, Stansfield (1985). *Secrecy and Democracy: The CIA in Transition*. Boston: Houghton Mifflin.

Wendt, Lloyd. (1979). *Chicago Tribune: The Rise of a Great American Newspaper*. Chicago: Rand McNally & Company.

Scholarly Articles

Anderson, F. M. (1912). "The Enforcement of the Alien and Sedition Laws," *Report of the American Historical Association.*

Blassi, Vincent (1983). "The Pathological Perspective and the First Amendment," *Columbia Law Review,* 85, 449.

Blodgett (1985, May). "Is it Espionage? Photo Leak to Media at Issue," *American Bar Association Journal,* 18.

Buckley, Susan (2002, March). "Reporting on the War on Terror: The Espionage Act and Other Scary Statutes" (Media Law Resource Center Report, N.Y.), *LDRC Bulletin* 2002:2.

Burkholder, Steven (1988). "The Morison Case: The Leaker as 'Spy,'" in *Freedom at Risk: Secrecy, Censorship, and Repression in the 1980s,* Richard Curry ed., 117-139, Philadelphia: Temple University Press, 1988.

Caroll, Thomas F. (1919). "Freedom of Speech and of the Press in War Time: The Espionage Act," *Michigan Law Review,* 621, 663.

Chafee, Zechariah Jr., (1919). "Freedom of Speech in Time of War," *Harvard Law Review,* 32, 932.

Cheh, Mary M. (1980, Jan.). "The Progressive Case and the Atomic Energy Act: Waking to the Dangers of Government Information Controls," *George Washington Law Review,* 48, 163.

"Developments in the Law: The National Security Interest and Civil Liberties" (1972). *Harvard Law Review,* 85, 1130.

Doyle, Kate (1999). "The End of Secrecy: U.S. National Security and the Imperative for Openness," *World Policy Journal,* 16, 34.

Duvall, Benjamin S. Jr. (1986). "The Occasions of Secrecy," *University of Pittsburgh Law Review,* 47, 579.

Edgar, Harold, and Schmidt, Benno C. Jr. (1973). "The Espionage Statutes and Publication of Defense Information," *Columbia Law Review,* 73, 5.

Edgar, Harold, and Schmidt, Benno C. Jr. (1986). "Curtiss-Wright Comes Home: Executive Power and National Security Secrecy," *Harvard Law Review,* 21, 349.

Elsea, Jennifer K. (2006). "Protection of National Security Information," *Congressional Research Service Report for Congress.*

Fuchs, Meredith (2006). "Judging Secrets: The Role Courts Should Play in Preventing Unnecessary Secrecy," *Administrative Law Review,* 58, 131.

Goren, Dina (1981). "Communication Intelligence and the Freedom of the Press: *The Chicago Tribune*'s Battle of Midway Dispatch and the Break of Japanese Naval Code," *Journal of Contemporary History,* 16, 663-690.

Gunther, Gerald (1975). "Learned Hand & the Origins of Modern First Amendment Doctrine," *Stanford Law Review,* 27, 719.

Hall, J. P. (1921). "Free Speech in War Time," *Columbia Law Review*, 21, 526.

Henkin, Louis (1971). "The Right to Know and the Duty to Withhold: The Case of the Pentagon Papers," *University of Pennsylvania Law Review*, 120, 271.

Kalven, Harry (1971). "Foreword: Even When the Nation Is at War," *Harvard Law Review*, 85, 3.

Marguiles, Peter (2005). "Above Contempt?: Regulation Government Overreaching in Terrorism Cases," *Southwestern University Law Review*, 34, 449.

Nimmer, Melville B. (1974). "National Security Secrets vs. Free Speech: The Issues Left Undecided in the Ellsberg Case," *Stanford Law Review*, 26, 311.

Note. (1942). "Legal Techniques for Protecting Free Discussion in Wartime," *Yale Law Journal*, 51, 798.

O'Brian, John Lord (1919). "Civil Liberty in War Time," *Reports of the New York State Bar Association*, 42, 275.

Sims, John Cary (2006). "What NSA Is Doing . . . and Why It Is Illegal," *Hastings Constitutional Law Quarterly*, 33, 105.

Stone, Geoffrey (1988). "The Reagan Administration, the First Amendment, and FBI Domestic Security Investigations," in *Freedom at Risk: Secrecy, Censorship, and Repression in the 1980s*, Richard Curry ed., 272-288, Philadelphia: Temple University Press, 1988.

Stone, Geoffrey (2004). "Wartime Fever," *Missouri Law Review*, 69, 1131.

Topol, David H. (1992). "*United States v. Morison*: A Threat to First Amendment Right to Publish National Security Information," *South Carolina Law Review*, 43, 600.

Trudel, Jereen (1986). "The Constitutionality of Section 793 of the Espionage Act and Its Application to Press Leaks," *Wayne Law Review*, 33, 205.

Unger, Stephen (1988). "A Proposal to Limit Government-Imposed Secrecy," in *Freedom at Risk: Secrecy, Censorship, and Repression in the 1980s*, Richard Curry ed., 94-102, Philadelphia: Temple University Press, 1988.

Warren (1918). "What Is Giving Aid and Comfort to the Enemy?" *Yale Law Journal*, 27, 331.

Weaver, William G., and Pallitto, Robert M. (2005). "State Secrets and the Executive Power," *Political Science Quarterly*, 120, 85.

Wells, Christina E. (2004). "Information Control in Times of Crisis: The Tools of Repression," *Ohio Northern University Law Review*, 30, 451.

Wigmore, John H. (1920). "*Abrams v. United States*," *Illinois Law Review*, 14, 539.

Historical Materials

Levy, Leonard W. (1985). *Emergence of a Free Press*. New York: Oxford University Press.

Lofton, John (1980). *The Press as Guardian of the First Amendment*, 102-115. Columbia: University of South Carolina.

Pollard, James E. (1973). *The Presidents and the Press*, 660-665. Octagon Books.

Power, Lucas A. Jr. (1991). *The Fourth Estate and the Constitution: Freedom of the Press in America*. Berkeley: University of California Press.

Rabban, David M.(1997). *Free Speech in its Forgotten Years*. Cambridge: Cambridge University Press.

Smith, Jeffrey A. (1999). *War and Press Freedom: The Problem of Prerogative Power*. New York: Oxford University Press.

Unger, Sanford J. (1972). *The Papers & The Papers: An Account of the Legal and Political Battle over the Pentagon Papers*. Syracuse, NY: E. P. Dutton & Co., Inc.

Winfield, Betty Houchin (1990). *FDR and the News Media*, 171-90. Champaign: University of Illinois Press.

Magazines and Newspapers

Adler, Jonathan, and Berry, Michael (2006, May 26). "Reporting Is Not a Crime," *National Review Online* (http://article.nationalreview.com/?q=NGExOD Y2ODliYzExYjNmZjZjYjAyNTM3NTg1NmQ5ZWU)

Bickel, Alexander (1972). "The 'Uninhibited, Robust and Wide-Open' First Amendment," *Commentary*, 54, 60.

Church, Frank (1985, Jan. 28). "Plugging the Leak of Secrets: New Efforts to Apply a 1917 Law Worry Civil Libertarians," *Time*, 45.

Freund, Ernst (1919, May 31). "The Debs Case and Freedom of Speech," *New Republic*, 19, 13.

"Government Secrecy Grows, Costs More, Report Says." (2005, Sept. 3). Associated Press.

Griswold, Erwin N. (1989, Feb. 15). "Secrets Not Worth Keeping: The Courts and Classified Information," *Washington Post*, A25.

Gup, Ted (2003, March/April). "Useful Secrets: In a Run-Up to War, How Do We Report Intelligently on Intelligence?" *Columbia Journalism Review*, 14.

Hentoff, Nat (2006, May 8). "Chilling Free Speech: AIPAC case raises questions," *Washington Times*, A18.

Lichtblau, Eric, and Shane, Scott (2006, Jan. 4). "Files Say Agency Initiated Growth of Spying Effort," *New York Times*, A1.

Priest, Dana, and White, Josh (2005, Aug. 3). "Before the War, CIA Reportedly Trained a Team of Iraqis to Aid U.S.," *Washington Post*, A12.

Parks, (1957). "Secrecy and the Public Interest in Military Affairs," *George Washington Law Review*, 26, 23.

Priest, Dana (2005, Nov. 2). "CIA Holds Terror Suspects in Secret Prisons," *Washington Post*, A1.

Risen, James, and Lichtblau, Eric (2005, Dec. 16). "Bush Lets U.S. Spy on Callers Without Courts," *New York Times*, A1.

Risen, James, and Johnston, David (2005, Aug. 18). "U.S. Diplomat Is Named in Secrets Case," *New York Times*, A22.

Rumsfeld, Donald (2005, July 18). "War of the Worlds," *Wall Street Journal*, A12.

Schoenfeld, Gabriel (2006, March). "Has the *New York Times* Violated the Espionage Act?" *Commentary*, 23.

Stone, Geoffrey R. (2006, May 8). "Scared of Scoops," *New York Times*, A21.

——— (2006, June 6). "The U.S. Can Keep a Secret," *Los Angeles Times*.

——— "The Espionage Bill," (1917, April 13), *New York Times*, 12.

Zelnick, Bob (2006, May 11). "Tenuous Free-Speech Claims," *Washington Times*.

18 U.S.C. § 798: Cases and Scholarly Articles

Buckley, Susan (2002, 2006 update). "Reporting on the War on Terror: The Espionage Act and Other Scary Statutes," Media Law Resource Center, at text accompanying footnotes 27-32.

Clift v. United States, 597 F.2d 826 (2nd Cir. 1979).

Edgar, Harold, and Schmidt, Benno C. Jr. (1973). "The Espionage Statutes and Publication of Defense Information," *Columbia Law Review*, 73, 930 at 1064-1069.

Elsea, Jennifer K. (2006). "Protection of National Security Information," *Congressional Research Service Report for Congress*, at 7-8, 14-21.

Lewis, Anthony (1987). "National Security: Muting the 'Vital Criticism,'" *UCLA Law Review*, 34, 1687.

Michalec, Mitchell J. (2002/2003). "The Classified Information Protection Act: Killing the Messenger or Killing the Message?" *Cleveland State University Law Review*, 50, 455.

Moon v. Central Intelligence Agency, 514 F. Supp. 836 (S.D. N.Y. 1981).

New York Times Co. v. United States, 403 U.S. 713, 735-137 (1971). (White, J. concurring, joined by Stewart, J.); Id. at 721 (Douglas, J. concurring).

Note. (1985). "Plugging the Leak: The Case for a Legislative Resolution of the Conflict between the Demands of Secrecy and the Need for an Open Government," *Virginia Law Review*, 71, 801.

United States v. Boyce, 594 F.2d 1246 (9th Cir. 1979).

United States v. Pelton, 835 F.2d 1067. (4th Cir. 1987).

Weaver v. United States Info. Agency, 87 F.3d 1429 (D.C. Cir. 1996).

Recent News Developments and Commentary

Babington, Charles (2006, June 30). "House GOP Chastises Media: Resolution Condemns Disclosure of Bank-Monitoring Program," *Washington Post*, A25.

Baquet, Dean, and Keller, Bill (2006, July 1). "When Do We Publish a Secret?" *New York Times*, A15.

Calame, Byron (2006, July 2). "Secrecy, Security, the President and the Press," *New York Times*, A10.

Chapman, Steve (2006, July 9). "Have Leaks Crippled War on Terrorism?" *Chicago Tribune*, (commentary), C7.

Cowan, Geoffrey, Jones, Alex S., Lavine, John, Lemann, Nicholas, Schell, Orville (2006, July 9). "When in Doubt, Publish," *Washington Post*, B2.

Dang, Dan Thanh and Kiehl, Stephen (2006, June 24), "Security vs. Freedom: Government, Press Grapple with Finding the Right Balance," *The Sun*, Baltimore.

Editorial. (2006, June 28). "Patriotism and the Press," *New York Times*, A22.

Editorial. (2006, June 29). "An Alert Press: Oversight of the Government's National Security Policies Is Needed Now More Than Ever," *Washington Post*, A26.

Editorial. (2006, June 30). "Fit and Unfit to Print: What Are the Obligations of the Press in Wartime?" *Wall Street Journal*, A12.

Editorial. (2006, August 27). "Secrecy and the Media," *Los Angeles Times*, M4.

Eggen, Dan (2006, July 29). "Grand Jury Probes News Leaks at NSA: Fired Officer Subpoenaed for Aug. 2," *Washington Post*, A2.

"Ex-NSA Officer Subpoenaed in Leaks Case." (2006, July 28). Associated Press.

Fein, Bruce (2006, August 22). "A More Secret Government?" *Washington Times* (Commentary), A15.

Gellman, Barton, Bluestein, Paul, and Linzer, Dafna (2006, June 23). "Bank Records Secretly Tapped," *Washington Post*, A1.

"Is the White House Scapegoating the *New York Times*?" (2006, July 2). *CNN Reliable Sources*, http://transcripts.cnn.com/TRANSCRIPTS/0607/02/rs.01.html.

Kurtz, Howard (2006, June 27). "Piling on the *New York Times* with a Scoop," *Washington Post*, C1.

Lewis, Neil A. (2006, July 19). "Bush Blocked Ethics Inquiry, Official Says," *New York Times*, A14.

Lichtblau, Eric, and Risen, James (2006, June 23). "Bank Data Is Sifted by U.S. in Secret to Block Terror," *New York Times*, A1.

Markon, Jerry (2006, August 11). "Judge Rejects Dismissal of Pro-Israel Lobbyists," *Washington Post*, A5.

"Media Refuses to Hold Surveillance Story." (2006, June 23). Associated Press.

Meyer, Josh, and Miller, Greg (2006, June 23). "Secret U.S. Program Tracks Global Bank Transfers," *Los Angeles Times*, A1.

"Now Congress Makes Moves against '*NY Times.*'" (2006, June 28, 2006). Associated Press.

Pincus, Walter (2006, May 22). "Prosecution of Journalists is Possible in NSA Leaks," *Washington Post*, A4.

———(2006, May 24). "Gonzales Defends Phone-Data Collect," *Washington Post*, A6.

———(2006, July 14). "GAO Finds Pentagon Erratic In Wielding Secrecy Stamp," *Washington Post*, A19.

Remnick, David (2006, July 3). "Nattering Nabobs," *New Yorker*, www.newyorker.com/talk/content/articles/060710ta_talk_remnick

Shafer, Jack (2006, March 9). "Bill Keller in Chains: Commentary's case for prosecuting the *Times* under the Espionage Act," *Slate*, www.slate.com/id/2137792.

Shane, Scott (2006, July 2). "A History of Publishing, and Not Publishing, Secrets," *New York Times*, sect. 4, 4.

Sheffield, Greg. (2006, June 26). "The Case for Prosecuting the *NY Times*," *News Busters* (Blog), http://newsbusters.org.

Sherman, Scott (2006, July 17). "Chilling the Press," *Nation*, www.thenation.com/doc/20060717/sherman.

Simpson, Glenn R. (2006, June 23). "Treasury Tracks Financial Data in Secret Program: Since 9/11, U.S. Has Used Subpoenas to Access Records from Fund-Transfer System," *Wall Street Journal*, A1.

Stolberg, Sheryl (2006, June 27). "Bush Says Report on Bank Data Was Disgraceful," *New York Times*, sect. A, 1

Stolberg, Sheryl Gay, and Lichtblau, Eric (2006, June 24). "Cheney Assails Press on Report on Bank Data," *New York Times*.

Stone, Geoffrey (2006, July 6). "Hamdan, NSA and the *New York Times*," *Huffington Post* (blog), www.huffingtonpost.com/geoffrey-r-stone/hamdannsa-and-the-n_b_24466.html.

Miscellaneous

Anderson, Kevin. "Examining DOJ's Investigation of Journalists Who Published Classified Information: Lessons from the Jack Anderson Case," Senate Judiciary Committee, June 6, 2006.

Ashcroft, John. *Report to Congress on Unauthorized Disclosures of Classified Information* (2002).

Bruce, James B. "The Consequences of Permissive Neglect," 47 *Studies in Intelligence* (2003).

Commission on Government Security, Hearings on Senate Judiciary Resolution 21 before the Subcomm. on Reorganization of the Senate Comm. on Government Operations, 84th Cong. 1st Sess. (1955).

Department of Defense Guide to Marking Classified Documents. DoD NISP Manual at 4-200, www.dss.mil/isec/ch4-2.htm (last visited Jan. 19, 2006).

Dinh, Viet D. "Memorandum of Law in Support of Defendants Steven J. Rosen's and Keith Weissman's Motion to Dismiss the Superseding Indictment" in *United States v. Franklin*, (E.D. Va. 2006).

Eastman, John C. "Does the First Amendment's Freedom of the Press Clause Place the Institutional Media Above the Law of Classified Secrets?" May 26, 2006 testimony before the Permanent Select Committee on Intelligence, U.S. House of Representatives.

Elsea, Jennifer K. "Protection of National Security Information," Congressional Research Service, (2006, June 30), www.fas.org/sgp/crs/secrecy/RL33502.pdf.

Espionage Laws and Leaks: Hearing Before the Subcomm. on Legislation of the House Permanent Select Comm. on Intelligence, 96th Cong. 1st Sess. 22 (1979).

Evans, Harry. *Secrecy vs. The Story*, www.newseum.org/warstories/essay/secrecy.htm (last visited May 12, 2006).

Executive Order No. 10290 (1951, Sept. 27), Prescribing Regulations Establishing Minimum Standards for the Classification, Transmission, and Handling, by Departments and Agencies of the Executive Branch, of Official Information Which Requires Safeguarding in the Interest of the Security of the United States.

Executive Order No. 12,958 (1995, Apr. 20), as amended by Executive Order No. 13,292 (2003, Mar. 28), (calling for more classified materials originally, however the amended Order curtails much of this and allows for more secrecy).

Feldstein, Mark. Statement for the Record, "Examining DOJ's Investigation of Journalists who Published Classified Information: Lessons from the Jack Anderson Case," Senate Judiciary Committee, June 6, 2006.

Friedrich, Matthew. Statement for the Record, "Examining DOJ's Investigation of Journalists who Published Classified Information: Lessons from the Jack Anderson Case," Senate Judiciary Committee, June 6, 2006.

Hearing Before the Subcomm. on Nat'l Sec., Emerging Threats and Int'l Relations of the House Comm. on Gov't Reform Hearing, 108th Cong. 82 (2004).

The Intelligence Community's Response to Past Terror Attacks against the United States from February 1993 to September 2001: Hearing Before the J.S. and H. Intelligence Comms., 107th Cong. 5 (2002).

Lapham, Anthony A. (1977, Mar. 18). *CIA Comments on Draft Unauthorized Disclosure Legislation and Related Matters.* Memorandum for PRM/NSC-11 Subcommittee Members, http://fas.org/sgp/othergov/lapham.html (last visited May 9, 2006).

Nelles, Walter (1921). *Espionage Act Cases* (pamphlet).

Nelson, Jack (2003). *U.S. Government Secrecy and the Current Crackdown on Leaks, in Terrorism, War and the Press,* published as Joan Shorenstein Centre on the Press, Politics and Public Policy Working paper 2003.

Presidential Directive on the Use of Polygraphs and Prepublication Review: Hearings Before the House Subcomm. on Civil and Constitutional Rights of the Comm. on the Judiciary, 98th Cong. 171-72 (1984).

Report of the Commission on Government Security (1957).

Report of the Joint Committee on the Investigation of the Pearl Harbor Attacks, 79th Cong. 2d Sess. (1946).

Schoenfeld, Gabriel. "Statement for the Record," Senate Judiciary Committee, "Examining DOJ's Investigation of Journalists who Published Classified Information: Lessons from the Jack Anderson Case," June 6, 2006.

———. Statement for the Record, May 26, 2006 testimony before the Permanent Select Committee on Intelligence, U.S. House of Representatives.

Smolla, Rodney. "First Amendment and Public Policy Issues Regarding Reporter's Privilege and Criminal Liability for Knowing Possession of Illegally Leaked Classified National Security Information," testimony before U.S. Senate Judiciary Committee on the Judiciary, June 6, 2006.

Stone, Geoffrey R. "Statement for the Record," May 26, 2006 testimony before the Permanent Select Committee on Intelligence, U.S. House of Representatives.

Turley, Jonathan. "Statement for the Record," May 26, 2006 testimony before the Permanent Select Committee on Intelligence, U.S. House of Representatives.

U.S. Government Information Policies and Practices—The Pentagon Papers, Hearings before a Subcomm. of the House Comm. on Government Operations, 92nd Cong., 1st Sess. (1971).

United States Government Accountability Office: Managing Sensitive Information— Actions Needed to Ensure Recent Changes in DOE Oversight Do Not Weaken an Effective Classification System (2006).

Willard, R. (1982, Mar. 31). "Report of the Interdepartmental Group on Unauthorized Disclosures of Classified Information, sect. B, p. 1 (unpublished report referred to in *United States v. Morison,* 604 F. Supp. 659 (1985)).

Congressional Attempts to Pass Sedition Legislation

108 Cong. Rec. 23140-41 (1962) (proposal by Senator Stennis to amend Section 279 of the Espionage Act to make disclosures of classified information a crime, without any narrow intent requirement).

National Security Secrets and the Administration of Justice: Report of the Senate Select Comm. On Intelligence, 95th Cong. 2d Sess. 18 (1978).

Report of the Joint Committee on the Investigation on the Investigation of the Pearl Harbor Attack, 79th Cong. 2d Sess. 252-531 (1946).

Index

obscenity: and prior restraint doctrine, 23
Ohio, 62n43
Oklahoma, 62n39
Oklahoma Press Publishing Co. v. Walling
(1946), 61n31
Oklahoma Publishing Co. v. District Court
(1977), 15n4, 26–27n8
Oregon, 62n43
Oxley, Michael G., 82

Pennsylvania, 62n43
Pentagon Papers, 19, 20, 21, 26n5, 35, 59,
70, 71, 90–91; and criminal prosecution, 22–23; and prior restraint, 22; and
public discourse, 25; public value of,
58; and Supreme Court, 20, 21, 22, 23,
24, 109. *See also* Daniel Ellsberg; New
York Times *v. United States*
Perry v. Sinderman (1972), 15n7
Phillips, Dickson, 89
Pickering v. Board of Education (1968), 8, 9,
10, 13, 16n11
Plame, Valerie, 59
Powell, Lewis F., 49, 50, 60–61n24
press, 4, 21; classified information, publication of, 19, 65; criminal prosecution
of, 24, 26; defining of, as anathema, 52;
and Espionage Act, 73; and government, 34; members of, determining of,
38, 39, 40; and national security, 96;
punishment of, 65; during wartime,
xiii; as watchdog role, xiii
priest-penitent privilege, 44n28
print journalism: as unregulated, 52
prior restraint doctrine: and First Amendment, 23; and Pentagon Papers, 22; as
questioned, 23; significance of, 23
private employers: employees, concessions
from, 7
privileges: argument against, 53; as attorney-client, 45, 47, 54, 56, 57, 58, 60n8;
benefits of, 54; and confidentiality, 58;
cost of, 54; as costless, 54; critical feature of, 46; as doctor-patient, 45, 47, 54,
56, 58; goal of, 45, 58; as journalist-
source, 47, 48; as priest-penitent, 45,

56; as psychotherapist-patient, 45, 46,
47, 56, 57; and public value, 58, 59; as
spousal communication, 45; and
whistleblowing, 58
Project on Government Secrecy for the
Federation of American Scientists, 79
public disclosure: communicative act, as
harmful, 33; and solicitation, 33
public employees, 21, 41n6; and classified
information, 9, 10, 12, 14, 17n27, 22,
31, 34, 37, 39, 65; nonclassification, as
dispositive, 17n19; punishment of, 37,
65; rights of, 12, 34; and unlawful disclosures, 27n9; and unlawful government conduct, 13, 14. *See also*
government employees

Randel, Jonathan, 88, 93
Rankin v. McPherson (1987), 16n11
Red Lion Broad. Co. v. FCC (1969), 61n36
Rhode Island, 59, 62n39
Roberts, Pat, 4n1, 83, 84
Roosevelt, Franklin D., 95, 96
Rosen, Steven J., 87
Rumsfeld, Donald, 84
Russo, Anthony, 90, 91

Schoenfeld, Gabriel, 87
Schumer, Charles, 81, 86
Seattle Times Co. v. Rhinehart (1984),
16n12
secrecy, 1; accountability, reconciling of,
22; national security, undermining of,
2; and wrongdoing, 2
security, 65; liberty, reconciling of, xiv
sedition, xiii
Sedition Act (1798), xiii, 68
Sedition Act (1918), xiii, xiv, 96
Sedition Acts: repeal of, 96
sedition laws, xiv, 95, 96
Senate Judiciary Committee, 80
September 11, 1
Sheehan, Neil, 35
Smith v. Daily Mail Publishing Co. (1979),
15n4, 26–27n8
Snepp v. United States (1980), 9, 10, 63n52

About the Author

EOFFREY R. STONE is Harry Kalven, Jr. Distinguished Service Professor of Law and former dean at the University of Chicago Law School. His book *Perilous Times: Free Speech in Wartime from the Sedition Act of 1798 to the War on Terrorism* (2004) received the Robert F. Kennedy Book Award for 2005, the *Los Angeles Times* Book Prize for 2004 as the Best Book in History, the American Political Science Association's Kammerer Award for 2005 for the Best Book in Political Science, the *New York Times* "100 Notable Books of the Year" in 2004, and Harvard University's 2005 Goldsmith Award for the Best Book in Public Affairs. Professor Stone is a member of the national Board of Directors of the American Constitution Society, a member of the National Advisory Council of the American Civil Liberties Union, vice president of the American Academy of Arts and Sciences, and a member of the American Law Institute.